Find The Balance

Find The Balance

ESSENTIAL
STEPS
TO FULFILMENT
IN YOUR WORK
AND LIFE

DEBORAH TOM

BOOKS

Published by BBC Books, BBC Worldwide Limited, Woodlands,

80 Wood Lane, London W12 0TT

First published 2004. Copyright © Deborah Tom 2004

ISBN 0 563 52138 4

Commissioning Editor: Emma Shackleton

Copy-editor: Florence Hamilton

Designer: Ann Thompson

Production Controller: Christopher Tinker

Set in Frutiger

Printed and bound in Great Britain by Mackays of Chatham

To Eliot Tom,
May your first glorious, happy, protected years be like the rest of your life. You are a total source of joy to your mummy and daddy. You deserve balance and fulfilment, my love.

Contents

Introduction

You have so much to gain from finding the balance …

Hello. I take it that if you have picked up a book with this title you are interested in finding a better balance in your life. Maybe your time is so taken up by the demands of others that you have none for yourself. Maybe your schedule is so tight that you can't dwell for long enjoying the company of a good friend or your family. Perhaps your work and family commitments are taking up so much of your time that you don't have the 'luxury' of time for other interests, such as hobbies. Maybe you know, deep down, that work has become omnipresent, that it even defines you, and that this isn't so wise or healthy. Maybe you are at a crossroads, keen to make things better and just needing to know the way. Whatever your case, this book will guide you by showing you some essential steps towards finding the balance.

In my work as a chartered psychologist, I have learned that we all want to feel fulfilled, want to feel that our life is worthwhile and a force for good. Out of the best of intentions we focus our energies and effort on our work, yet if this is to a degree that is out of balance with our other human needs it backfires on us. The false promise of personal wealth, material possessions and status as the measures of success and the route to happiness has misled and seduced many, and a wide body of recent research has confirmed what many of us are now discovering. The value system that puts single-minded focus on acquiring money and status is faulty; it simply does not lead to happiness and feelings of contentment. Unless individuals are living in real poverty, money will only marginally improve their feelings of well-being. Fulfilment is not about what we can get, it is about what we experience and what we give. Fulfilment is about connecting. If we are not in the right place, with the right people, using the best we have to offer we will feel lonely, disconnected and withdrawn. That is why work–life balance, at its most philosophical, is important. We need to work out what is important to us, where, how and with whom we want to connect, and to organise our lives around this.

It takes moral courage to create work–life balance but we have a right to lead a fulfilled life and a right for that to be respected. The balance we achieve will vary at different stages of our lives. There will be times when the scales have to tip in one direction or another in order to guarantee better balance later. What's important is that we are conscious of this at the time and that we make a choice about our values and priorities, negotiated around the values and priorities of other people in our lives.

In thinking about your work–life balance, be reassured that you are not alone. This is a growing concern shared by many. People from all walks of life are feeling the pressure: too much to do, too many decisions to make, too little time. There is the subtle yet pernicious pressure from being always accessible through mobiles and e-mails. There is the pressure of running a family and home with both parents working, or the onerous workload of being a single parent. There is the pressure of one partner being the home-maker while the other partner is working crazy hours. It is a serious issue because long working hours can result in feelings of irritability, anxiety and depression and thus impact negatively on our relationships – our connectedness with others.

In the US, Japan, Netherlands and Scandinavia research has shown links between working long hours and heart disease. A European-wide study by the European Foundation for Improvement of Living and Working Conditions found that 'intensification' of work has risen sharply in the last ten years. We are working faster and under the pressure of tighter deadlines than ever before and at the same time juggling increasing home demands.

■ Responsibility to yourself and others

A recent Mental Health Foundation report found that working long hours clearly had a negative impact on personal life and mental well-being. The national work-life balance survey carried out by the charity found that as we work longer hours we spend even more of our 'free' time thinking or worrying about work. In this study, half of the participants reported that long working hours were responsible for making them feel irritable. A quarter of the participants reported feelings of anxiety, and a third suffered from depression: all from the same cause. These and many other facts and statistics paint us a strong picture of our need to take the responsibility to create time: for ourselves, for our friends and families, for rest and relaxation, and for attention to our health and well-being.

We spend most of our lives at work. As employers and governments are just waking up to the value of flexible working in retaining staff and preventing sickness, so you need to empower yourself to find a balance that works for you. There is widespread agreement within the boards of blue-chip companies and research and government establishments on the need for more paid parental leave, wider opportunities for part-time or new ways of working and a curtailing of the long-hours culture. For example, men are increasingly encouraged to take an active role in parenting and given protection from discrimination if they ask for flexi-time – although in practice the right to ask is no guarantee of organisational compliance. There is proof that good working practices positively affect the bottom line: they can be of real financial benefit to a company. When good practices related to work–life balance are implemented – such as help in providing care for dependents, flexi-time, more individual control over the working environment – productivity, staff retention and staff creativity go up and absenteeism goes down. So the reasons are both moral and economic.

If you need more time with elderly relatives or young children, if you need time for self-development, time to think or rest and simply enjoy life – you need the skills to negotiate this. You need to work to create a plan, a plan that takes into account yours and others' particular needs and values within the realms of practical possibility, and then you need to negotiate to put the plan into action. This book will help you do that.

■ What this book can do

This book is designed to offer you an easy-to-use, accessible resource that will help you take a fresh look at what matters to you and bring more of a balance into your life and work. To lead a successful life, we need to be honest with ourselves about what we need and what we value and who we really want to be. It is a brave move to face up to your true identity, particularly if it goes against the ideas and roles others have in mind for you. It is my intention to both support and challenge you in taking this step.

You will be looking at what work–life balance means for you, what you really want, and what your needs, aspirations, intentions and goals are. You will analyse your strengths and weaknesses, the opportunities and threats, all as part of formulating your plan, whatever it might be. You will learn how to implement the practicalities, and how to sustain and develop your vision. There will be guidance and strategies on making a start, help and encouragement in making your commitment, and constructive suggestions of how to share the vision with others in your life so that this isn't an isolated dream but a practical plan with the support it needs to succeed.

The exercises in this book are designed to help you review the aspects of your life that might be out of balance, and encourage you to find ways of addressing the imbalance and bringing about change. This will help you develop the kind of skills you need to communicate constructively in situations where you need a positive outcome. I will also encourage you to take the time you need to make the transition. Towards the end of the book are case studies that show you how possible it is to make changes, to develop flexibility or to adjust so that your needs are being met and you have more control over your life. Lastly, there is a resource section to help you find useful information.

As you work through this book, you may be inclined to skip the exercises or particular topics – if this happens to you, the chances are that these are the areas that really need some attention, so I urge you to take your time and do the exercises and dwell on the topics … it could be just what you need to help you towards success.

In establishing a better work–life balance, there is much to gain. Qualities such as social responsibility, interconnectedness, generosity and peace of mind have a chance to develop. The pursuit of balance will be of benefit not only to you but also your immediate environment and, indeed, society as a whole.

Ask yourself
what is actually
happening now

Chapter 1
The meaning of work–life balance

❏ Find out why balance is important

❏ Assess your level of job satisfaction

❏ Think about change

❏ Develop the skill of awareness

This first chapter will explore with you why and how you want to rebalance your life and where you want to place your energies. It may be a challenge to create a new way of living and working, but the process of finding the balance will enable you to feel the benefit from the moment you begin.

▒ Why balance is important

Many people are waking up to the fact that fulfilment is not necessarily about material possessions and social status – the Aston Martin, the second home in the sun, the next promotion, the third child or trophy partner – although for some these things seem to be essential and are the reasons why they put most of their time, energy and effort into work. If you ask people who are happy with their lives to tell you their secret, however, they will probably say that life is not about what you want, what you can get – it is about what you can contribute. Finding work-life balance, whatever that means for you, includes what you give as well as what you get in return. If you want to find fulfilment you need to look to give fulfilment. Ask yourself, 'Why am I here?' rather than 'What do I want to get?', and the answer is more likely to lead you to real, lasting fulfilment. Here are some of the benefits to be gained from a balanced existence.

A wide social life and varied interests help give us perspective. Perspective acts as a buffer against stress, enhances our resilience and increases the likelihood of making good decisions.

Rest and recreation balanced coupled with productive work seem to create a healthier body and mind. Going without either for long periods tends to lead to disrupted physical and mental well-being.

Happiness in midlife and later depends on having done something that you consider is worthwhile, and having loving and supportive relationships. You don't get to a place of having stable secure relationships unless you invest attention, time and effort in them.

Taking care of your body and mind pays off in keeping you fit and healthy and looking your best – and it pays greatest dividends when you're post-50.

■ Assess your job satisfaction

Our work environment is often where we spend most of our time; ideally, it is where we are at our most creative, and often it is where we have our closest friends, meet our partners and feel valued. Our very identity is often closely linked to our work. A lot of us love our work and this is just as well – we are spending more time at work than with our children, our partners, our friends, our places of worship or in nature.

If you spend most of your time on one activity, you can't find any meaning in your work or you feel work is taking over your life, you may need to create more of a balance. Sometimes we may choose to tip the work–life balance in favour of work because we have a desire and ambition to achieve a particular goal. If the balance has shifted from choice – and we remain the driving force behind it – then our personal enthusiasm and positive energy will keep us going. The trick is to ensure the scales do not remain tipped one way for too long.

It has been observed that 'life satisfaction' has risen slightly since the 1990s, but 'job satisfaction' is not as attractive to people as it once was. The price you pay for success at work is now being evaluated in terms of the stress and ill-health it can cause. What does job satisfaction mean when you examine it closely? How can you assess what sort of satisfaction you get out of your work? It is worth taking some time to think about this – the chances are it's time you reviewed exactly how satisfying your job is, and what satisfaction is all about. Research by Peter Warr suggests there are ten features of the working environment that create job satisfaction. How does your work measure up? Space has been left for you to write down your thoughts.

1 Do you have the opportunity for personal control and autonomy?

....

2 Do you believe that you have ample opportunity to use your best skills?

....

3 Do the demands of the job match your skill levels?

....

4 Is there the right amount of variety in the tasks you perform to keep you interested, not bored or overwhelmed?

....

5 Is there enough job security for you to feel reasonably safe?

....

6 Do you have enough income to keep you from poverty?

....

7 Are there measures to ensure appropriate physical security?

....

8 Do you have a supportive boss?

....

9 Is there enough opportunity for the right kind of social interactions?

....

10 Does your work give you a valued social position?

....

■ Me Ltd

Linked to work is your sense of who you are. What do you get out of work besides income? Think of yourself as Me Ltd, with a corporate strategy based around the following:

your vision
your mission
your values
your life interests
your assets
your stakeholder interests

This is all part of putting work in perspective: getting work working for you.

■ Where are you at?

You might already be starting to get an idea of what work–life balance means to you. For some it is about finding time to spend with family and friends. For a single person it might be about making time to meet a potential life partner and consider establishing a family. For others it is about having the opportunity to pursue other activities, interests or aspirations – to reconnect or discover a part of themselves that is not defined by work, or parenthood.

Maybe you simply feel tired from too much work and don't have the energy you would like to have for other areas of your life. Maybe you feel stuck, stressed, under pressure, anxious and low in energy; you think something has to change, but you're not quite sure what or how. Maybe you dislike your present job, feel that you have got into a rut, as if there must be something more to life, but can't pinpoint exactly what it is. Is there pressure from outside? Perhaps others are telling you that you should want something which you don't, or that you should – or shouldn't – be satisfied with the life you have. Perhaps others want something from you they are not getting.

Or maybe you got what you wanted. It is possible to achieve personal fulfilment after gaining something that you have striven for and made sacrifices for. But can you see when you have achieved what you wanted and then stop your efforts and enjoy the outcome? Are you able to see the effect of your striving on those around you? Did you bring the people in your life with you? Is their balance out of kilter as a result of your ambitions? Will they have to pay a price for your success in the short or long term? What are the benefits to them (non-material as well as material)? Is it worth it for them? Is it worth it for you?

Whatever your scenario might be, if you could use some help in reviewing where you are at right now, some information on workable techniques and skills, a little help with decision-making – read on, and remember that work–life balance is something millions of people are dealing with right now. Even if you just have a vague sense of dissatisfaction, a feeling that you could be giving more and receiving more, you are not alone.

Finding work–life balance is fundamentally about having enough energy left over to feel as if you *have* a life, of which work is just one part! At a certain point you will need to begin to reflect on how you measure achievement, success and failure. Success isn't always what it seems, and sometimes what looks like failure is actually an opportunity for renewal.

■ Facing change

Sometimes there are catalysts, or triggers, that force us to look at ourselves and our lives. Sometimes changes happen that are not in our control and we need all our resources to make adjustments that will enable us to maintain our physical and mental health while we move through them.

Do you sense a forthcoming crossroads in your life? Are you in the midst of starting a new career, losing a job, having a child, ending a relationship or moving to a new city? Every life includes periods of personal transition: a shift of focus, a shift in attitude, a shift in lifestyle – a shift in life balance. This may involve decisions about whether to work full-time or part-time, whether to set up your own business, adapting to illness or redundancy, coping with relocation or starting a family. No-one but you can say whether the realignment you need to make in your life is big or small. No-one but you can name the emotion it conjures up.

Sometimes, in the face of big changes, it can feel like a sudden decision is being made when in fact the work has been in progress for months, if not years. You might have been thinking, imagining, preparing, waiting for a long time to take some action and make the decision known. Change affects us all differently – for some a house move is fun, for others a nightmare; for some a career change is exciting, for others unsettling. Be careful not to pre-judge how you are managing any shift or change.

■ Time to reflect: awareness and perspective

In finding balance you need to be conscious that it involves choices, priorities and values. Exercises later on in the book will help you clarify and review your values; you'll need to apply some discipline in remaining steadfast to them. If you feel as you start out that finding the balance that's right for you is tough-going, be reassured that you probably have already exhibited many of the strengths and skills you need to help you make good life choices.

Research in positive psychology has shown us that certain attitudes and practices act as buffers against the stress, anxiety and depression all of us will face at some time in our lives. These attitudes and practices are awareness, courage, a perspective on the future, optimism, interpersonal skills, a faith, a good work ethic, hope, honesty and perseverance. These are not only positive qualities, but also practical skills that everyone can learn, and we will explore them in more detail later in the book.

Let's make a start at clarifying what changes you want to make, why and how. To be clear about what is actually going on in your life (as opposed to what you think might be happening), *awareness* is perhaps the most essential skill you can cultivate. There is a very simple way to do this at any moment in the day:

> *simply bring your attention into the present, notice how you are breathing, where any tension is, and name how you are feeling.*

Keep doing this whenever you notice your mind running over past or future situations, scenarios or fantasies.

The task of getting a perspective on your life and work – the subject of the next essential step – will begin to appear to be much easier. So take a conscious breath and ask yourself: what is actually happening now? Reflect on where you are now that you have thought about what has been raised in this chapter, and decide where you need to find more balance in your life and work. But first, take a few moments just to relax. This will help you to open your mind to what might be possible, and prepare the way for the review, clearing, planning and preparation that you will need to do later on.

You can work it out –
sometimes you have
to take a chance
on life again

Chapter 2
Taking stock:
a new perspective

❏ Decide what your needs are

❏ Define success and achievement

❏ Assess what works/what doesn't

❏ Take more control

Sometimes things happen that make us look at what's really going on in our lives. Sometimes it is a life event that forces us to stop and reflect on what's out of balance. Maybe we are at last facing up to feelings we have been hiding from, or to the fact that we are not as healthy as we would like to be. If we just stop being so busy and quietly take some time to be with how we feel, it is more difficult to get away from the truth, and while it might be uncomfortable, you know it makes sense! Are you overworking, going to the gym all the time or keeping your eyes glued to the television in an attempt to forget or deny what isn't right in your life?

■ Catalysts for change

Reflect on the following possibilities. How would they affect your life? How would you deal with such changes? How are you reacting emotionally to each possibility? What do you feel as you consider the implications of each one for you, your family, your security, your physical and mental health?

redundancy or the sack
being headhunted unexpectedly
falling in love
losing a big contract
finding out about new training possibilities
inheritance
children leaving home
divorce
following a partner abroad
illness which means you can't work full-time
marriage
company relocating 500 miles away
promotion

■ Decide what your needs are

The humanistic psychologist Abraham Maslow's well-known theory of human needs and fulfilment outlines the basics as food, shelter, water, safety, stability and security, both physical and psychological. Then there is a sense of belonging, of affiliation, of love, followed by self-esteem that stems from achievements, respect and recognition. Ultimately we have what Maslow called 'self-actualisation' – the stage at which you fulfil your potential – although Maslow himself believed that this depended not so much on material achievement as on an inner experience of value and meaning. New research across four continents has found the four basic psychological requirements that are necessary in order for us to feel fulfilled:

> robust self-esteem
> a sense of autonomy
> belief in and use of our competence
> relatedness with others.

Take some time here to consider how you define success, and how this might differ from the kind of achievement that you feel might be expected of you. Consider where you are on the four basic psychological needs.

For all of us, money is fundamentally important to happiness and fulfilment – if you don't have enough to eat, a secure place to live and the means to keep warm in the winter, you are unlikely to feel that life is satisfactory. Once our basic needs have been met and financially we have what we consider necessary to provide a comfortable life, however, we don't necessarily feel fulfilled – instead, we often crave more. Ask yourself why you are constantly looking for a rise in your salary, your turnover, your profits. If you know that ultimately it only marginally increases your happiness, persisting with that kind of behaviour might start to look like a bad old habit.

■ A new perspective on your life

If you feel you have 'a good life' the chances are you:

> like your life
> feel as if you are working towards a valued aim
> enjoy reasonable health
> have enough food to eat and a secure place to live

have friends who support you emotionally and are good to be with
are intellectually stimulated and have some autonomy at work
have a loving, close, reliable long-term partner
have a fulfilling sex life.

Learning the skills we need for living a good life is something we usually start to do only when we realise that something has become unmanageable. Many people make choices based on what they might get out of them, what sounds good at the time. Psychologists have found that people are really bad at guessing and at making decisions based on what we think will make us happy. As a result, there is a tendency to over-invest in material things because we forget that we will soon be so used to them that they give little pleasure or satisfaction.

The way we look at life is the important thing in determining whether we feel our life is in or out of balance. Most people grasp at things – the job, the house, the partner – hoping to find fulfilment, and realise instead that everything is forever changing.

■ The wheel of well-being

Give some thought to how much you like your life. Would you say your life was balanced? Do you feel you are working towards a goal you value?

Are your emotions recognised, are they shared, are they looked after? Or are you bored, thwarted, avoiding, waiting, isolated, wanting?

The wheel of well-being is a tool that will help you review your life. Use it to identify what is working for you and what isn't. It is divided into seven sections, as follows:

work/career
finances/income
health/well-being
religion, spirituality or philosophy
personal development
love life
friends/social/recreation

In each section, give a score of between 1 and 10. If you are currently completely satisfied with your love life put 10 in that section. 5 is fair to middling, and 1 is not at all. Use the numbers in between as well. If in some categories you are satisfied with some aspects and unsatisfied with others, write down 5, and try to identify the areas where you are satisfied and those where you want to see some improvement, development or growth. Use the wheel to:

assess the current balance in your life – what's working and what isn't
celebrate where and how you have achieved balance and fulfilment
define your needs and your values as a foundation for setting goals.

Spend some time now writing in your scores.

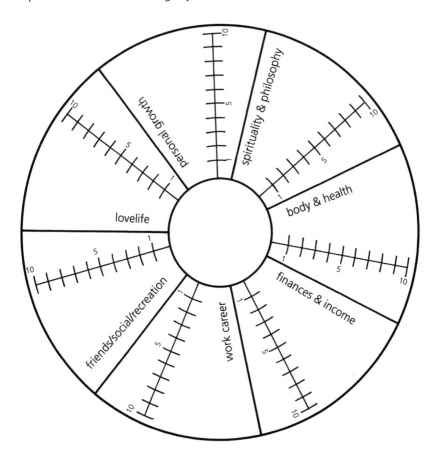

Consider and reflect. Don't forget that you can keep coming back to the chart in order to review progress. If you want to change a score, do so.

Wherever you put in a low score of 1–3, think about why this area is so unsatisfying. Ask yourself what you can do about it. Where you put 4–5, ask yourself why the score isn't higher, and what more you could do. Where you put 6–10, be specific about what is working there for you.

Take a look at your wheel – does it look balanced or imbalanced?

What do you think and feel about what you see?

....

What are the consequences of the low scores in your life?

....

Are you investing too much in the high scores – are they overshadowing lack of balance? If so, you need to ask how much this bothers you.

....

Where would you like a different balance in your life?

....

How has the situation that you see arisen? Why else?

....

How would you like it to be?

....

■ Visualise a better balance

Take a moment to inhale deeply and relax as you breathe out. Imagine yourself a year from now with a better balance in your life. What do you look like, sound like, feel like – see yourself going about your life engaging with others, and from that better place imagine yourself twice as satisfied again with the balance in your life. Imagine yourself, life-size, walking and talking in that place.

Take notice of what you look like now, sound like, feel like and – step into that picture of yourself and from those eyes see what you see, listen to your voice and how others are responding around you and feel how much better you feel.

Can you name the feeling?

Can you be even more explicit about what that feeling is?

That's your pay-off for realigning your world into a better balance.

■ Identifying stress

Stress is a word that covers a multitude of emotional and physical responses to stuff that happens to us in life. We are all under stress some of the time; it covers everything from irritability to anger to depression, from frustration to out-of-control exhilaration, from annoyance to overload. Sometimes stress causes complex feelings, that is, not 'just' anger or 'just' depression. Later in the book we will explore stress management in detail – for now, just begin to explore any symptoms you might have that could be stress-related.

Try to describe how you are feeling. Notice if you have any aches, pains or tension and in what specific parts of your body. If you have more than one or two of the following responses of stress, you need to stop, take some time out for yourself and explore the root of what you are really feeling. Circle any that you are experiencing, reflect on what might be causing you to feel stressed, identify the responses and think about which stimuli caused them. Be aware of what triggers stress responses in you, and which responses in particular.

irritability

sweating

rapid heartbeat

twitching

tense shoulders or back

irritable bowel

listlessness

crying

insomnia

angry outbursts

too much casual sex

too much alcohol

finding it hard to concentrate

feeling isolated from people who love you

What are the causes? Where do you need help? Who can you ask for help?

■ Performance anxiety and burnout

At work we are often asked and expected to reframe problems into 'challenges' and 'opportunities' – to think positively and achieve maximum performance at all costs. Over time, working under intense pressure can lead to you feeling edgy, overwhelmed, and can result in frequent headaches, migraines, back problems and other stress-related illnesses. Many employees do not question the decisions, pressures and stress they are put under because they fear that if they did, their position and prospects might be jeopardised. People often know that working long hours is damaging their helath and relationships but they feel they can't risk working fewer hours in case they fall behind with their workload. It is only recently that overworking has begun to be recognised as a serious problem, one that reduces productivity and can result in a company losing talented people.

Some companies are now introducing health management training sessions aimed at encouraging their employees to lead healthier lifestyles, thereby enabling them to achieve more. At some point, however, *you* have to find a balance between your personal values and what is expected of you in your career. The drive to work and earn more, become a high achiever and find success at the top of your profession may be what keeps you going. But for many people the consequences take over almost without their being aware of it. Burnout is a real problem and its consequences can be serious. It starts when you find yourself taking on too much. Maybe you are excited about your work, maybe you have had too much work over a long period, or circumstances are such that there is just a lot to do. This is when you have to make choices and be realistic about the consequences of those decisions. These are the symptoms of approaching burnout:

You wake up as tired as you went to bed

You have a vague sense of wanting to avoid others

You are using stimulants to get yourself going

You have lost inspiration or, at least, it doesn't come on demand

You feel depressed even though things are going well

You end the day with absolutely nothing left to give.

The natural repercussions are often that you get to a point where you don't care any more, you feel demoralised, work loses its meaning and you may feel isolated from other aspects of your life. The very thing you focused all your attention on as so important now feels like nothing. Has the price of success been too high? That is what happens when your priorities and your values are not in balance. Maybe the demands of your job are unrealistic – maybe you need to find the courage to tell your superior that the workload cannot be achieved without too much being sacrificed on your part.

When you've invested and given too much in one area, it takes courage to admit that your life might have got out of control. Sometimes this feeling can come after a major disappointment – like a partner leaving you or losing your job. It is important to remember that you are much more than any past failure, more than a mere role or a title. Your ego, although battered, your soul, although wandering, your gifts and your virtues, although maybe not appreciated in the past, are still there, and they can be put to good use again.

It is important to care for yourself, in order for you to have the resources in you to care for others. Women who work and look after a family are especially at risk of spending too little time on themselves. Self-employed people seem to have a good chance of being happy with their work–life balance. One in five are very content with their balance, strikingly more than any other category. Perhaps more than any other group they decide their working time and have a reasonable degree of autonomy and control over when, where and how they work. How much time do you give to yourself? How much time do you give to the multitude of tasks that need to be done, to others' needs, others' demands? What does it cost you to care for everyone but yourself?

You can work it out. You are good at coping. You have adapted in the past well. Just for starters, remind yourself of something you have coped with in your life and write it down, right now, right here:

....

....

■ What is in or out of balance?

As you begin really to get down to some work on finding balance, this questionnaire will help give you a preliminary picture of what is out of balance and where you need to put your energies in order to bring about the shifts or changes that you need. Tick the measure to reflect where you are for each set of questions.

PERSONAL DEVELOPMENT

I feel I'm not using my mind enough	-3 -2 -1 0 1 2 3	I have to use a lot of creative thinking in my job
It's a long time since I learnt any new skills	-3 -2 -1 0 1 2 3	I am using my skills every day in the work I do
I'm not really sure what I want to do, I just feel stuck	-3 -2 -1 0 1 2 3	I'm interested in my development and read lots of inspirational books
I feel as though I have stagnated	-3 -2 -1 0 1 2 3	My knowledge is increasing all the time

HEALTH

Sometimes I feel unfit and unhealthy	-3 -2 -1 0 1 2 3	I feel fit, vital and in good health
I don't have time for sport or exercise	-3 -2 -1 0 1 2 3	I enjoy walking, swimming and activity holidays
I find it difficult to eat healthily every day	-3 -2 -1 0 1 2 3	I ensure that I eat fresh fruit and vegetables daily
I often feel stressed and anxious	-3 -2 -1 0 1 2 3	I do relax easily and find a way to relieve stress

SOCIAL /FRIENDS/ RECREATION

| I rarely see my friends | -3 -2 -1 0 1 2 3 | I am in regular contact and have fun with my friends |

| I have no really close friend I can confide in | -3 -2 -1 0 1 2 3 | I have a couple of really close friends I confide in |

| I do not seem to fit into a social group | -3 -2 -1 0 1 2 3 | I feel very comfortable with my social group |

| I don't mix well or have a wide social circle | -3 -2 -1 0 1 2 3 | I mix well and have a wide social circle |

| I don't have much time for recreation | -3 -2 -1 0 1 2 3 | I make sure I have rest, recreation and a laugh |

LOVE LIFE

| I don't express my feelings | -3 -2 -1 0 1 2 3 | I feel free to express my feelings |

| I would like someone special to love and love me | -3 -2 -1 0 1 2 3 | I enjoy the love of some-one special to me |

| People close to me do not like my partner | -3 -2 -1 0 1 2 3 | People close to me like my partner |

| My sex life feels dull and unexciting | -3 -2 -1 0 1 2 3 | I enjoy a rewarding and satisfying sex life |

| My main relationship is not secure or nourishing | -3 -2 -1 0 1 2 3 | My main relationship is healthy, deep and good |

FINANCES

I am in debt   -3 -2 -1 0 1 2 3 My bank balance is healthy

I have no savings or -3 -2 -1 0 1 2 3 I have savings and a good
much pension   pension

I want to earn more -3 -2 -1 0 1 2 3 I am pretty content with
than 3 times what I earn   what I earn

I have no cushion if I -3 -2 -1 0 1 2 3 I have enough to cushion
do not work   any run of bad luck

The lack of money -3 -2 -1 0 1 2 3 My financial state is safe
worries and depresses me   and secure

RELIGION/SPIRITUALITY

I have no faith/religion/ -3 -2 -1 0 1 2 3 I am religious; I have a
spiritual practice   spirituality/philosophy

My faith sometimes -3 -2 -1 0 1 2 3 I am resolute and com-
leaves me   fortable with my faith

There are conflicts in my -3 -2 -1 0 1 2 3 I am in a group where
faith and others' around me   my faith is shared

I don't mix well or have -3 -2 -1 0 1 2 3 I mix well and have a wide
a wide social circle   social circle

I do not feel connected -3 -2 -1 0 1 2 3 I sense a connection with
with a higher self/soul   my soul/higher self/others

■ What about now?

If you were asked to describe how you feel at this moment, would you say:

relaxed
uncertain
happy
cynical
tired
excited
agitated
in pain
glad
interested
curious.

Be as specific as you can. Explore what is going on in your mind and be aware of any physical sensations that might help you describe how you feel – such as sore eyes, nausea, sweating, headache, coldness, neck pain; are you frowning, biting your nails, or do you feel comfortable? If you need to, move around, shift your position, get up and open a window, have a stretch, go out for a walk, or get a glass of water. Try bringing some flexibility into the time you spend reading and working through this book. If there is tension or pain in part of your body, acknowledge that this is part of your search for balance. Whatever happens, try to keep an open mind.

■ How good would better balance be?

Be as creative as you like in trying to answer the following questions.

What do you think you want/need to achieve or change in order to find more of a balance?

What will greater balance give you?

What do you think the disadvantages might be?

Does this make you want to pursue finding a balance or forget about it?

Do you feel anxious just thinking about making any changes?

■ Where can you be more creative?

Productivity is usually related to work-based output, and it is also about creativity. With a bit of creative thinking, you might find that suddenly you feel like putting more energy into areas where some balance is needed. Creative thinking is a skill that everyone can use by just taking a different view of things – what you might see from a window at the back of your house can look very different from the view at the front! We might develop a different view of success from the usual wealth and status definition; we could take a more exploratory approach to what we seek, what we focus on, where we spend our time. Working flexible hours, working part-time, becoming self-employed: all have different implications depending on our personal situation, but what seems impossible one week might look more likely after you spend some time discussing ideas with those close to you: family, friends, work colleagues, contacts, neighbours.

The most productive people tend to be those who take a proactive view of their lives, who make opportunities to engage with their environments, and who gain pleasure in the experiences of life. There's no doubt that some work is hard, repetitive and low paid. However, it's true to say that no matter what work you are doing – whether it is gardening, writing, cleaning toilets, addressing a conference, wheeling a patient into an operating theatre, negotiating a business deal, presenting a TV programme or doing voluntary work at a day-care centre – there are ways of connecting to the work in terms of its overall value, of introducing some creativity into what you're doing and of calming the mind. Many people talk in terms of 'flow': the experience of being fully engaged in what you are doing.

Some people create flow wherever they are, in whatever role. These are phrases that express some of the qualities of a state of flow:

Engagement in interactions with others
Challenge that exercises your skills
Mental focus
Creativity with a sense of play about it
Complexity
Work becomes fun, pleasurable, motivational
Values and sense of integrity: being able to do the work that
matches your values.

■ Not enough time? Do less!

Many people live with a gnawing sense of anxiety because they have lots of work to do that is incomplete. The average executive, research shows, has 300 hours of incomplete work to do. We clutter our minds with what we must do, should do, could do. We also give ourselves undue stress about it – there really isn't enough time to do it all and when we don't we begin to doubt ourselves, lower our sense of self-worth and feel frustrated with ourselves or resent others. If you are in this state, you need to clear out the clutter, simplify your life. Something as simple as clearing your desk or workspace helps creates that much-needed space in your head too.

Someone recently pointed out to me that when we die we will still leave behind an in-tray and bills will arrive months after we have passed on. We can never complete all our work, so perhaps what we need is to adopt an attitude of not letting it bother us so much.

■ Trust and listen to your intuition

If you realise you are not living the life you want, be easy on yourself. It's all right to feel like this because once we realise we are in a place (literal or metaphorical) that's not where we want to be – our soul will force us to do something about it. Much of your strength and good decision-making will come to you naturally from your innate qualities or character if you are willing to stop, calm your mind, be still and just listen.

You may be someone who finds endless opportunities to do different jobs, make lots of money, to win – and get caught up in it all. You might find, however, that what excited you once has now consumed you. It is in control of your life. What started out as a thrill has turned into a manic habit of 'busyness'. Hard as it is to admit it, many of us who are seemingly 'together' are actually much less in control than we like to think we are. Ask yourself for some spontaneous answers to these questions:

What really matters to me? What is important?
What do I really care about?
What am I most interested in?
What do I really enjoy?

How much of what I enjoy is in my life?

What can I do about that right away?

What can I do to change things longer term?

■ You can control the pace of your life

You can control the pace of your life, indeed you must, you have to – or some-one else will. There are many ways of orchestrating a successful life according to your values and particular circumstances. If you are self-employed and work from home, you may need to make sure you don't become isolated. If you are the sort of person who works best in extended periods of focused concentration you will need to allow yourself extended periods of recuperation and socialising to gain a balance. Ultimately, the state of your health, your conscience and your relationships are what counts when you sum up the worth of your life.

If you want to learn how to take control of the pace of your life, it helps to know when and how you need to say 'no' in a constructive way. If you are feel-ing overworked and stressed, ask yourself what is important to you. At some point, you are entitled to assert your need for space, for balance, for renewal and rejuvenation. It is vital that you are brave enough to not take on more than is manageable – more than *you* can manage. The chances are you won't seize up, you won't be forgotten about or passed over. You will stand out as someone of character, someone who dared to go against the crowd in order to do the right thing, someone who has worked out their life's priorities and placed them firmly in their diary. Only you know how you feel. If you are operating on low energy, you will not be able to give your best. Having the courage to say no can set a wonderful example to others.

■ Build your support networks – they can help

Many of us face the challenge now of having to move away from parents, family and friends in order to find a job. If you are willing to be flexible about where you work, this could mean moving away from support networks that currently enable you to feel resilient, fulfilled and supported. Research points to the fact that towards the end of your life, when you look back, you will believe you had a good life if you negotiated a balance that accommodated your achievements but also suited your values and your primary social relationships.

Sometimes having too much choice actually causes distress. As we have more options of different lifestyles, we have to face the difficulty of making decisions to do with juggling work, family and children. If you are facing a big job move, it can be energising and exciting if you are a naturally outgoing person. However, if you are on the shy side and slow to settle into a new environment, be sure that you don't put everything into the new job and isolate yourself socially – connecting with others is an essential part of work–life balance.

Status and wealth are not good measures of personal well-being. Sometimes passing up promotion is the route to well-being. Knowing when to ask for help, and realising when it is time to give up something that has been important in your life, is a sign of wisdom. Resilience, determination and perseverance are important qualities in times of change. And our society is changing fast; our mothers' and fathers' rules for living do not always make sense now. We are having to make it up as we go along much of the time. We need to find the courage to confront what doesn't seem to be working, ask the big questions and be more creative in looking for and finding the answers. See your choice not as stressful but as a way of exploring your real purpose.

■ Developing positive partnerships

We are creating new rules, new expectations and new responsibilities as we go. Two working parents may both enjoy the social and mental stimulation at work, the money, and the separateness as they are able to live out parts of their lives as individuals, but this arrangement can take a toll on the relationship. Each is under pressure to participate in housework and childcare. For men this might be a fairly new demand, as most full-time working women now believe that the housework should be shared. Men often leave home at 7.30 to return home 12 hours later. A recent UK survey in *Management Today* showed that 30 per cent of men said that their job 'seriously interferes with their private life'. A remarkable 96 per cent of men found their work interesting and challenging and were happy to be playing a role in the upbringing of their children. Still, men hesitate to fight for flexi-time to be with their children more. Only 9 per cent of men work part-time, while 43 per cent of women workers are part-time. If you work for a small firm, that flexibility may not even be on offer.

If you have children, you will want to spend a lot of time with them. Your children's future sense of well-being, their creativity and their ability to lead others depends on how much time you spend with them and how well you look after them in the first two years of their lives. And children want their parents to be less stressed, even if it means seeing them less. Try asking your child or a child you care about what they like doing best with you. My daughter said, 'Playing board games with you.' I had to ask myself, 'Board games? Now when was the last time I did that?' Listen to what the child in your life says, and keep asking.

Finding and maintaining a work–life balance is still the biggest barrier to women reaching their potential. Even if you work in a progressive company with policies in place that allow flexibility and mobility, the attitudes of your managers may hinder you from taking them up. Women are under a lot of pressure in the long-working-hours culture as they continue to do the lion's share of household labour and organising children's schooling activities and family social activities.

After divorce many women feel as if they've become a single parent while their ex-husband has returned to being a bachelor. Some men like it that way, while others wish to engage more with their children but perhaps don't have the access they feel they'd like. Children, of course, are aware of the animosity and the absence, no matter how hard parents try to hide it. They can adapt to parents not being there, but at a cost. For everyone in a situation like this, striking the right balance is especially important.

■ Connecting with others – and yourself

In achieving a balance in your life and work, you will find it helpful to spend some time doing 'inner work' in order to really get to know what your personal resources are, and how they might help you. You don't often get an opportunity to explore the quality of your character. For example, how do you rate yourself on kindness, generosity, compassion, a sense of humour, having a lively, open and active mind, an ability to give without expecting a reward or approval? The intellect might convince you and those around you that you like your lifestyle and believe you've done quite well, but to find out how you truly feel you need to sit still and listen to what is in your heart. As you work through this book, practise the art of listening to your heart as you begin to review your life and work and make decisions, plans and choices about what needs to change in your life to give it more balance. Here's an experiment which will show you the value of taking small steps, even if they might at first seem unconnected with the bigger picture or the greater goal. However, please don't try this if you are tired because you have been giving too much to others already. You cannot do it if you are exhausted. Take some to look after yourself, pamper yourself and find a place where you can be nourished to rebalance before you do this exercise. Then, during the coming week, try this:

> *Deliberately and consciously do something purely for your own pleasure. Write about the experience, how you are thinking and how you feel the next day.*

> *Do something to show some kindness to someone else in an act that calls upon your strengths and virtues. Write about your act of kindness the next day; what you experienced, felt and thought about it.*

> *Try to keep both of these about level in terms of intensity and duration.*

Before moving on to the next chapter, which will encourage you to explore further how you see yourself and the world around you, take some time to reflect on what you have learnt so far, and how useful this is to you.

It's not what you do
but the way that
you do it that matters

Chapter 3
Developing self-perception

❑ Appreciate the good things in your life

❑ Behave as if you are making a difference

❑ Bring your values into the work you do

❑ Enhance your self-esteem and confidence

You may well need to make changes in your life; you may want more for yourself and for others, but how are you doing with what you already have? Could it be that you actually need to stop accumulating in order to feel that you are on the right track to find balance in your life? A review of where you are right now will help you take a fresh look at yourself and your situation. This chapter is designed to enable you to explore further which aspects of your way of managing your life and work might be improved. This will help you to clarify where you need to make changes – you might even be surprised by some parts of the picture that emerge as you work through the themes.

What are you grateful about in your life right now?
Where do you feel blessed?
What are you appreciative of?
What gives you joy in your life right now?
What gives you pleasure in your life right now?
What comforts you in your life right now?
What excites you and makes you feel alive in your life right now?
What makes you feel good?
Where in your life can you throw back your head and laugh?

If you ask yourself these questions often you will find they empower you, charge you, put some sparkle in your eyes. Every time I am stuck in a traffic jam, for example, every time I feel down or disappointed, every time I have an important meeting, every time I need to be something for someone that I am not feeling at the time – these act as a kick-start into a genuinely good state. You don't have to fake a smile or put on a stiff upper lip; you can simply access the things in life that lift your spirits – the people, places and activities that please and nourish you and put you into a better frame of mind.

■ Choose how you feel

Choosing the way you feel is the subject of many personal development books. As far as achieving a work–life balance is concerned, it is an essential part of the self-perception and self-management process that will give you the motivation you need to make changes. The way you perceive something is created by reframing techniques and you can choose the way you feel by changing your focus, your beliefs or your attitudes. You can choose to change how you relate to a situation, the way you feel about it, or your proximity to it. Of course, this doesn't mean changing another person or changing an actual situation (for example, losing a job, a business going into liquidation or your boss dying). Perception involves taking into account the enigmatic forces of intuition, curiosity, fascination, commitment, passion, 'flow', motivation, focus, compulsion, duty, loyalty, faith and acting on your sense of calling. Your sense of fulfilment can be increased dramatically by tomorrow morning if you simply say to yourself:

It is not what I do but the way I do it that matters.

Behave as if you can make a difference, are making a difference, *are* the difference, and ask yourself a couple of questions:

What do I value, what are my principles and how can I show more of them in my decisions and behaviour?

How can I show my appreciation and gratitude?

▇ The importance of your values

Knowing your values and living your life according to them is the path to your authenticity, your power and your honesty, qualities that often get left out of self-assessment exercises. Values are what you believe in – they are part of your character. If you are living out someone else's values, or the conventional values of the society you live in, and don't feel that you go along with them – don't be surprised if you feel stressed. Having to live up to values you don't entirely believe in is difficult for anyone.

Of course, you have to know your values in order to live according to them. Typically, when I ask a group of people if they know what their values are and can prioritise them, very few know how to respond. Many people spend a large part of their time making decisions, interacting with others, unwittingly leading and influencing others, yet they aren't conscious of their values.

Principled leaders do more than speak about their values: they act according to what they believe in. Values are enduring, and serve as guides that allow people to respond rapidly and flexibly to events around them (although major life events and transitions can result in values changing). Not surprisingly, being strongly connected to your values produces happiness and mental health. A positive mood is infectious, felt and caught by people around you. Examining your virtues is an important task in your journey, creating energy and positivity around you – essential resources in your search for work–life balance.

The following exercise is an easy-to-use personal development tool that will help you clarify what values are important to you, and you can use the results to develop your own character and motivation skills. Write in the first column someone's name, in the second the qualities you appreciate in them, and in the third a 'one-word' value. If you get stuck, read the top of the next page first.

Person	Qualities	Value

▓ Understanding your values

To fill in your value chart, you might use people you work with, your friends and peers, a child you know, a counsellor or helper you are involved with, family, bosses, celebrities, and political and spiritual leaders. You might admire Nelson Mandela for his courage, dignity and integrity, for example. And you might admire his courage above all: so that's one of your values.

Now consider the following questions:

What do you want to be remembered for?

What do you respond best to in others?

What do you want others to respond to in you?

What do you prize, and what does that say about your values?

What do you enjoy, and what does that say about your values?

What do you love, and what does that say about your values?

What is your favourite film, and what does that say about your values?

What is your favourite book, and what does that say about your view of predicaments and solutions?

Who do you love, and why?

Who do you want to be like, and why?

Whose advice do you take, and why?

Who do you listen to, and why?

What makes you feel good, and what does that say about your values?

Who is your role model – what do you like about them? How are you like them and how different?

What magazines do you like – what does that say about the environment you like to be immersed in?

What do you like to do in your leisure time and what does this say about your self-expression/role/rewards?

What motto would you use to title your life story?

You should now be in a position to work out your top three values. List your top three values here:

....

....

Now consider how you can live more authentically in relation to your values by asking yourself the following questions:

What should you keep doing?

What should you stop doing?

What should you start doing?

Who do you know who shares your values? (This will tell you if you are in the right company.)

Which value is most clear from the way you live your life?

Which value is not clear from the way you live your life?

What gets in the way of living your values? (E.g. do any of the values clash; is there conflict between values?)

At what cost to yourself and others?

What could you do about it? (E.g. if the values clash, where is there room for negotiation, for influence, for compromise?)

■ Setting out to achieve success

Optimism and extroversion are personality traits that are often correlated with feelings of happiness and fulfilment. Some people are naturally inclined to be happier than others as a result of their genetic inheritance and brain chemistry. The brain chemicals serotonin and dopamine are linked with reported happiness levels, and neuroscientists have found that genes play a role in regulating these. However, everyone can learn skills that will help cultivate motivation, discipline, planning and organising abilities – all of which will help you feel more optimistic about your future and broaden the possibilities that you feel are open to you.

What blocks you from being more who you want to be? How do you feel about these:

Speaking up at work when you are asked to do something you don't think is right

Asking for an overdue salary increase

Covering up someone else's mistakes

Helping someone who is being bullied or victimised at work

Running your own business.

■ Understanding your blocks

Now take some time to think about what your blocks might be. Are you, for example:

> Neglecting something or someone?
>
> Feeling that nothing you can do will make any difference?
>
> Waiting for something to happen?
>
> Hoping someone else will do it?
>
> Distracted by something else?
>
> Feeling afraid or angry?

Think about what you are blocking and how you feel about it. For example, do you put off doing any exercise, then feel guilty and lethargic?

When people are upset with you, what might they say? 'How could you forget that? I thought I could rely on you.' Or something entirely different?

What happens if you don't live according to your values? Do you go quiet, withdraw, stop communicating? Do you feel compromised, uncomfortable, disappointed in yourself? Or what else?

Now that you've started thinking about blocks, get a pen and some paper and write down the ten obstacles, deficits or demons that get in your way at home and at work. Be as specific as you can: 'I worry about making a mess of a presentation'; 'I'm afraid of hurting others by telling them what I need.' Whatever applies to you.

■ Reframing a situation

Reframing is a useful technique that enables you to see something from a different perspective. It is especially helpful in situations where there is conflict, lack of understanding and breakdown in communication, and can bring about real improvement and resolution. There are five steps.

Step 1: Name a situation in the past where things didn't work out that well and you were culpable because your behaviour got in the way of a better result.

For example: *I know I should have reprimanded a staff member who has been bullying someone in the office, but because of other considerations I decided not to and now the situation is worse.*

Step 2: Acknowledge your irrational fears about your own capability. Work out what it is that is blocking you.

He might get mad and form allegiances with other members of the team and they would all exclude me.

Step 3: What did you do that wasted your own time or got in your way of being productive?

I procrastinated, worried and half-heartedly tried to talk to the staff member without any clear objective in mind.

Step 4: Find the opportunity to feel good by listing your strengths and values and see how they could help you take a step towards knocking down that block.

I have shown courage and commitment in the past. I am sure of my own judgement in this case and I also have the back-up of another, trusted colleague.

Step 5: What is the positive benefit in taking action? What do you, and others, have to gain?

I will feel more authentic and there will be closure either way. As things stand, he knows I am unhappy and do not trust him as much because I have withdrawn from him and have queried his judgements and movements in a way I haven't before, so the relationship is not good now. Things can only improve by the action.

In taking action I will demonstrate my own courage. I will show my respect for others: a key value for me. To encourage myself I will remember when I've done the right thing in the past, and I will think of the inspiring examples of other people. I will start communicating in the most clear, calm way I can: 'You know how I value respect for others in this department. Well, something you have done has disturbed me ...' I also believe this will be to his benefit in the long run, and good for the department, as well as for the victim of his behaviour.

■ Don't miss your chance

Stress and pain are always a sign that we are holding on to something – and that something is often some notion of ourselves. When we feel not quite up to dealing with something, a little inadequate perhaps, we hold on tight and get a bit mean-spirited. By facing your demons and practising generosity, you can give and let go simultaneously. As a result you open up, loosen up and lighten up.

It's worth remembering that missed opportunities figure more predominately in people's regrets than any particular action they might have done.

You can always benefit from making the most of any opportunity, even if it's only to smile at someone as you pass in the corridor, no matter how insignificant it might seem at the time.

What opportunity are you forsaking?

What would you regret not doing?

What do you need to let go of in order to do it?

What can you do that takes you in the direction you want to go, is a small risk that can be safely taken?

What small changes can you make to do more of the things you love and that you know do you good?

As you commit to doing your work more mindfully, conscious of your impact and the consequences, you will find more enjoyment in doing it. It is possible to learn to love what you have to do, but if you really cannot name any part of the work you do that you enjoy, then it's likely that this is where you need to start making changes.

Acknowledge now the bits of your work and life that you love or like to do, and begin to feel gratitude for being able to do those things. If this seems difficult at first, try to keep an open mind and just practise it for a while – you might find you begin to feel grateful for some aspect of your work, even if it's only a small thing. If not, now is the time to think about going – because staying in a job that gives you no satisfaction at all is bad for your health.

■ Making changes

At the beginning of any process of making changes most of us ask ourselves countless questions, sometimes the same one over and over again. We believe that we need certainty; that we need to be absolutely sure about what we are doing. However, if you remember that there are no fixed guarantees and that complete certainty is impossible, you might find it easier to move forward.

For example, you might be asking questions like these:

> Am I doing what is right for me?
> Should I change career direction?
> Why am I doing this?
> Should I have kids? Do I want them?
> Am I with the right partner? Is s/he the one for me? Would I be happier on my own or with someone else?

But the answers to questions like these are not simple: there is no totally perfect partner waiting for you, no absolutely ideal job, and, especially, there isn't only one 'you' waiting to be realised, resulting in total fulfilment and a guarantee of a lifetime of happiness! Rather, there are lots of possibilities to be explored, experimented with, analysed and practised to find out how they fit in with your soul's idea of what your life lessons might be.

There is an interesting ancient saying: 'The circumstances of your life reflect the needs of the soul', which you might find is worth some thought, no matter how you define 'soul'. Soul, of course, means many different things to different people – I define it as the essence of 'you' that you know is there, the you that is contained, whole, quite distinct from and yet connected to other people. Your soul stays constant but it can find many different personas and lifestyles in this life: the personality finds many ways to express itself. The personality that is *you* has to decide which lifestyle, which job, which role and persona you need to adopt in your unfolding life story. Self-perception is a skill that we all need, not just in times of change but throughout our lives.

■ Feelings about change

As you begin to get to grips with what you need to do in order to achieve balance, you might find that you are reacting in ways that are designed to protect and defend you from change. A lot of people fear change because they fear losing what they need, want and value about the way part of their life and work is currently shaped. Contradictory feelings about making changes are quite common – usually fear kick-starts a reaction, a defence, a denial, a distraction, diversion, an attack, a running away from, an avoidance.

Fear is often nothing more than False Evidence Appearing Real – a concept that features in much personal development work. For example, say you have been made redundant once in your career and have just joined a company which, it turns out, is in financial difficulty. You start to lose sleep worrying about the possibility of another redundancy, but this doesn't necessarily mean the same thing is going to happen again. You are suffering from F.E.A.R.

How often have you realised that something that caused you to feel fear was unfounded? An upsetting thought can depress our mood; instead of dropping it, we hold on to it and file it away with other related unhappy, disappointed, it-never-works, demoralised, low-energy thoughts – and before we know it, we are on a downward spiral into negativity. Then we might get agitated, irritable or try to distract ourselves somehow. We pivot between depression and agitated anxiety. It is easy to escalate negative feelings by elaborating or exaggerating them and letting our emotions take control of our mind and body. This is how things get out of proportion, and if we allow free rein to out-of-proportion worries we might find ourselves in trouble, either alone with no support network or having compromised those who might support us.

Ask yourself about your reaction to something that is unsettling you. Explore whether your approach is one of enquiry and exploration, a search for balance and perspective, firmly grounded in reality. Or do you feel you are on an emotional roller-coaster, acting up or acting out with very little control over the outcome?

If you are grappling with an incident that didn't go well, mulling over your own bad behaviour, dealing with disappointment or a person who seems difficult, watch what is happening in your mind and be sure that you aren't slipping into old habits, beliefs, ways of behaving and attitudes towards others and situations that are not serving you well in the here and now.

Ask yourself where the lesson in this is for you.

■ Understanding how your past is affecting the present

Everyone carries around a personal life story that provides an identity and comes with all kinds of mechanisms for protecting and defending the persona. You tell yourself how successful you can be, what your limitations are, what you can achieve, who you can trust, what role you have to play – even what sort of people you can make friends with.

These beliefs and habits of mind are rooted in our emotional memory and are usually experiences or things that were said to us in childhood and then reinforced at various times in our lives until they became quite rigid ways of seeing ourselves and who we think we are. We are usually unaware that they are actively affecting our attitudes and behaviour. They tend to be insidious and tenacious, and can result in our feeling stuck without being able to clarify exactly what is preventing us from having more choice, more control over our everyday lives. We may not want to feel so limited, but we seem to be powerless to make changes to do with our sense of choice, our personal power and our ability to behave differently.

There is a way that you can get off this treadmill and start looking at alternative possibilities in your life. Working your way through this book, you can give yourself the opportunity, the time and space, to take a look at these beliefs and see how true they are and how useful they are to you. Where they are not serving you well in the present, let them go. Begin to do this in the context of your situation now, as you go about finding more balance in your life and work. The following exercises are not about the past, but about how you are *now*, in the present – the only time you ever have.

■ Reviewing your capabilities

A very important aspect of self-perception is your sense of your own capabilities – your beliefs about what you can and cannot do. This provides the most authentic evidence of what your personal resources are to enable you to succeed in what you do. Interestingly, we also need to experience failure to build resilience, although too much failure early in life can hold us back, until we make a conscious effort to leave the past behind and live in the present. This might seem simplistic, but as many people know from experience, as soon as we do this we have a clear field in which to learn how to create new habits, change outworn beliefs, and start to take more control over our life and work.

As well as making judgements about our capability, we also believe that we know what we are worth – or not. Self-esteem is about the judgements you make about your sense of worth. There is no essential correlation between how you judge your capabilities and how much you like yourself – you may not think you can do something very well but do not suffer any loss of self-esteem because you do not invest your esteem into that activity. For example, you may see yourself as someone who doesn't need to learn how to use the office photocopier, so you don't connect the ability to make photocopies with what you feel you are worth – and with luck there will be someone whose job it is to do this instead! You ideally gravitate towards something that gives you a feeling of self-worth and raises your self-esteem, and this tends to lead to you doing work that you are good at and feel good about.

■ Seeing things as they really are

Start this enquiry by looking at how much of a friend you are to other people and to yourself. You might see yourself as special, or you might feel less entitled to success than someone who, say, has a private income and does not need to work hard to earn a living. You might feel you are superior to the person who does your photocopying. Do you have friends who are in less skilled, perhaps low-paid jobs, who are much older or younger than you are? How fixed is your self-image and what might this mean for your work–life balance project? Imagine you are suddenly faced with redundancy, unemployment or a salary cut. This enables you to work part-time to care for an ageing parent or spend more time with the children, but think about how the reality of the change in status would affect your self-perception.

Self-image refers to the overall picture you have of yourself, for example, your national and cultural identity, social role, physical appearance, likes and dislikes, personal qualities. Take me, for example: I am English, white, a professional psychologist, a mother. I am short; I like Genesis; I am compassionate.

Self-confidence refers to our sense that we can do things successfully. Self-worth and self-esteem reflect the overall opinion we have of ourselves and the value we place on ourselves as people. Self-esteem has two interrelated aspects: it entails a sense of personal efficacy and a sense of personal worth. It is the integrated sum of self-confidence and self-respect. It is the conviction that one is competent to live and worthy of living. Self-esteem is related to positive mental health and psychological well-being, and good personal adjustment to ageing/change/relationship building.

In order to make positive choices and changes in the future, it's important to let go of old habits and beliefs. You don't have to continue to reflect other people's prejudices, preferences or negativity. You are capable of creating your own self-image every minute of the day. If you work through this book with a sense of what is really going on, instead of what you wish might happen, it will offer you a chance to create and maintain self-esteem and self-confidence in terms of who you are now, what your needs are and where you are putting your energies and effort.

■ Reviewing your self-esteem

Have a look at some of the things you need to change in order to find a more balanced way of living and working. Consider what might be holding you back and needs to be brought up-to-date and into the present. You can change the way you behave, and therefore the feedback that will impact on how you think and feel about yourself, which, again, will impact on the way you behave. The process is a circular one, not a linear progression.

Low self-esteem is related to anxiety and stress, exploitative relationships, low goals and lower attainment. It is an important factor in how you go about achieving work–life balance – and the good news is that it is dynamic: it can change.

To find out about the condition of your self-esteem, have a look at the following statements. Do they apply to you?

My experiences have taught me to value myself
I appreciate my good qualities
I accept my weaknesses
I have mostly met my parents' expectations and the standards set for me
As a child I received a lot of praise, affection and attention
I can make myself feel better after difficulties
I am comfortable asking for other people's attention and time
My parents never or rarely smacked or abused me
I have reasonable expectations of what I can achieve
I fitted in quite well at home and school
I am kind and encouraging to myself, rather than self-critical.

■ How self-esteem develops

Our self-esteem originates in a social and family context. No single factor is overwhelmingly significant and nothing in a child's development is causal or deterministic, but there are predisposing factors.

1 Parental involvement

Attachment and bonding clearly have a significant affect on our self-esteem. These are some of the questions you may wish to consider. Were your parents absent at any time in your early childhood? Did they show love and attention or did you have a sense of indifference? Did they give you lots of hugs, tell you they loved you, showed you plenty of respect by being firm and fair – or not? Did they delight in your strengths and forgive your weaknesses? Did your mother have naturally high self-esteem? (Children model and imitate their mother's self-esteem, so if it is low or she is depressed then children's self-esteem is lowered too.)

2 Values

Our schooling and early family life teach us pro-self-esteem values, such as. courage, self-discipline, honour, caring. What values or principles did your early schooling, your immediate family and those you respected teach you?

3 Social group

Self-confidence is often set by comparison and identification with friends or peer group. What group did you identify with; how was their self-esteem?

4 Gender differences

Women tend to attach their self-value to how they are valued or seen by others. Men tend to attach their self-value to how competent or successful they are.

Does this ring true for you? What have been the repercussions of this in your life?

5 Personality

Generally optimistic and autonomous people have higher self-esteem. Are you optimistic? Do you tend to see the upside first, or the downside? Do you have some independence and autonomy in your life?

If your self-esteem is low, ask yourself:

What or who is eroding my sense of personal power?

Where can I and how can I reinforce my sense of power?

Why am I feeling insignificant here?

How can I be more significant?

Have I crossed one of my own moral standards?

Where can I get feedback on my competence?

Sometimes low self-esteem can drive a person towards success because of a fear of failure – such as, the workaholic over-achiever. Think about how your self-esteem has been a driver or a hindrance in your life and work so far.

Do you suffer from any of these symptoms of low self-esteem?

Do you have a negative self-image, sometimes feeling inadequate or unattractive?

Do you become distressed and deeply disappointed after being criticised?

Do you get flustered, exhausted, very tense under pressure?

Do you imagine failure and feel very aggrieved when things go wrong?

Do you get prickly, defensive and or aggressive if challenged or pushed?

Do you struggle on with head down not wanting to get noticed?

Are you unlikely to ask for other people's opinions on how you're doing?

Do you allow your needs to be thwarted by others' needs?

Questions to help you access higher self-esteem:

What do you like about yourself, however small and fleeting?

What are some of the positive qualities you think you possess?

What are three of your achievements, large or small, that you can readily name?

What challenges have you faced and overcome?

What do other people like about you?

Understanding your self-talk

It is very important to be aware of the messages you are giving yourself. You may not always be aware of where all the messages come from, but think of some of the things you say about yourself and work back from there. What have people told you about yourself? We all have negative and positive comments from our past that either directly or indirectly affect the way we see ourselves. Write the comments that contribute to your self-esteem and put a + (positive) or − (negative) sign next to them.

If most of the statements you hear are negative, you need to let go of those and replace them with positive statements, such as compliments, praise, acknowledgement and gratitude from friends, colleagues, peers and bosses who know what you are really capable of, believe in you and trust your judgement.

As you engage in the exercises in this book, take some time out of 'doing' and examine where you are going and who you are 'being' along the way. To get the most out of these exercises, you need to get up close and personal with yourself. You are entitled to be comfortable with yourself, live your life according to your values, make decisions and put your energy into finding a balance of work and life that suits your particular needs, circumstances and values. It's worth investing your time and energy into achieving this.

Being different can give you an advantage

In his recent book *The Gift of Dyslexia*, Ron Davis has linked the roots of dyslexia with those of Attention Deficit Disorder, autism and hyperactivity. Thomas Edison, Alexander Graham Bell, Leonardo da Vinci, Walt Disney, General George Patton, Winston Churchill, Jackie Stewart and David Beckham all have symptoms of dyslexia as thus defined. People with dyslexia use multi-dimensional thinking involving all the senses, which is quicker than 'verbal' thinking (and is akin to intuitive, very fast cognition). Sometimes they are seen as 'daydreamers'; they can get disorientated quickly, and while this could be seen as a disadvantage, it can be a source of creativity. Once they have experienced something they pick it up at a deep level, and know how to do things almost instinctively without seemingly thinking it through thereafter. It is worth looking again at what you think you do that annoys others or you think gets in your way and reframing it to ask, 'Where could this be useful, how could I use it creatively?'

■ Enhance your self-esteem

If you feel your self-esteem could do with a boost, ask yourself:

Who helps your self-esteem?

How can you spend more time with these people?

Where can you find more opportunities to be around the things that spark an upward trend in your self-esteem?

■ Life scripts

The concept of a 'life script' originated in the US human potential movement. A script is really about self-perception and can be changed. It is not fixed or rigid, but is based on a collection of beliefs and attitudes absorbed early in life, often from parents, teachers or family situations. A script contains all the ways of behaving that we are attached to and identify as 'ours' – a blueprint for our idea of 'who we are'.

Your script includes what you believe you are capable of, what you think you deserve, what your possibilities and limitations are. Your script can restrict you or encourage you in your life and work, and can also provide a set of rules for social etiquette that varies according to nationality, class, culture, and how we see ourselves within the social structure. Some people seem to be born with an innate talent or gift for music, art or acting, for example, and they are happy to spend their lives using their creativity in that field – they may have taken on an inherited 'script' and wouldn't dream of doing anything else.

For most people, though, it takes time to work out what you want to do in life, and you may not have the financial support or encouragement that you believe you need in order to succeed. But if you really believe you can be a champion ice skater, say, and if you focus all your energies on getting where you want to be, the chances are that nothing will stop you from achieving your goal. Our life scripts affect how much success we can have, whether we ought to have children and how many, where we can live. They can even be applied to table manners, to what is a socially acceptable way to sit, speak, or interact with other people.

If our self-concept, or 'who we are', seems to be threatened, the perceived threat activates 'a self-limiting fear', something we rarely talk about or even acknowledge but which can be a frequent unconscious driver of behaviour. As we go through life, our scripts either match or mismatch others'. All of us at times overreact to something that seems to have hit a raw nerve. If you find yourself on the receiving end of this kind of reaction you can be sure you have unwittingly and innocently defaulted against someone else's script and they react defensively to protect themselves from what they see as an attack.

Most people have their own 'rules for living' that protect them from people transgressing their self-limiting fears. Usually, however, someone accidentally hits one of our triggers and the whole script is unconsciously played back to us and we react not to their stimuli but to our own self-limiting fear. Even if their 'attack' was mild, we often overreact because self-limiting fears evoke a strong emotional survival instinct in us.

How scripts and triggers work

Early life experiences, such as criticism, indifference, lack of respect, neglect, abandonment and abuse can lead to self-limiting fears when you conclude what you are and are not, what you can do and what you cannot. For example, you might think, 'I am not as smart or pretty as my mother'; 'One day people might find out I am not that capable'; 'I must work harder than everyone because I am not that clever'.

To allow you to cope within your belief system you develop strategies, which could be known as Little Life Rules: 'They won't notice me unless I am funny', 'I must do better to be admired', 'I mustn't cause a fuss or I will be made to look stupid'. Sometimes, though, our self-limiting fears are triggered. Triggers are situations that mirror early experiences, even though you are living within your own little life rules. Examples of these might be being made redundant even if you have been working very hard; being dumped in a personal relationship even though you worked hard to look good and not make a fuss, being usurped in promotion even though you have been doing everything well.

■ Getting over your self-limiting fears

To overcome your self-limiting fears you need to understand what they are and how they affect you. One way to do this is to start by listing them. Then, consider how each one of them affects you. Ask yourself the questions overleaf.

What situations, things, people act as triggers for you?

What are the anxiety feelings and thoughts you experience?

How do you behave at times when you feel like this?

What are the consequences of that behaviour?

How else could you behave more constructively?

Now take one situation in which you have found yourself in some difficulties. Try to break it down in the following way.

Name one fear it produced for you.

Name one negative feeling it produced.

Name one negative thought it produced.

Name one alternative positive thought you now think
you could have had.

Name one different way in which that positive thought would have
made you feel.

Name one, small, different behaviour you could have employed or done
which might have produced a more positive result.

■ Examining your little life rules

Let's examine some of your rules for life. Write in the space on the page:

I must

....

The people who work for me must

....

Life must

....

A little rule for living I have is

....

It has impacted on my life in this way:

....

I have this rule because

....

The rule is no longer useful because

....

The pay-offs for the rule have been

....

The penalties of the rule have been

....

A more realistic and helpful rule could be

....

What are the types of thing you like about yourself (however small)?
List at least three qualities:

....

....

....

What are some ways you could employ what you've learned about
    scripts, triggers, little life rules?
Write down three possible ideas:

....

....

....

You are getting
ready to break
the impasse

Chapter 4
Focusing on priorities

❏ Being more than your behaviour patterns

❏ Small changes can give you work–life balance

❏ Focus on the present

❏ Put energy into endings

We all have a personal style in how we respond to others and react to events in our life. Recent brain research shows that the brain, the personality, our values, beliefs and the patterns of our behaviour can and do stretch, adjust, adapt and change throughout our lives. While genetics, brain structure, family traits and inherited life patterns and values play a huge part in how we develop from infancy, the mind's capacity is still under-used.

Scientific research into human consciousness has a long way to go before it can explain the power of the human mind. The fixed and separate entity we think we are is mostly a collection of accumulated identifications and attachments which have become solidified over time. It is possible to free oneself from limiting patterns of behaviour. There are many instances of how people in their teens, adolescence or adult life have transcended the most traumatic early experiences and gone on to lead successful lives.

Related to work–life balance, this means that no one has to stay 'stuck' in a familiar role or way of life and there are tried and tested techniques and skills for changing the way you see things – a slight shift in perception can make a huge difference. Patterns of behaviour are often looked at and categorised in psychometric questionnaires. It is useful to see your preferences, your typical behavioural patterns or, at least, how you thinks you behave. Always remember, however, that all they show is how you see your typical behavioural patterns – this is not the whole you. You are much more than your habits and patterns.

■ Looking after yourself

If you are in a state of mind where you know that a change is due, you may be reluctant to make the decisions and begin working out your plan of action. Some of us respond to the need for change with fear, confusion, apprehension, self-doubt, dread, worry, fury or a host of other emotions. Sometimes there is also longing, excitement, impending relief. You may be fighting off the moment of reckoning by keeping busy, being especially pleasant to others, avoiding something; you may be sharper than usual, may feel sad, lose your temper or feel low in energy.

At this time, by all means consider others but you must first look after yourself. Employers can encourage a culture of openness about time constraints and workload, but individuals need to take personal responsibility for work–life balance, which means, for example, speaking up when work expectations and demands are too much. Later in the book we will look at the importance of health and well-being in more detail. Meanwhile, if you are not respecting, valuing and caring for yourself you will not be able to do the same for others without feeling resentment, jealousy or anger. If you are quietly thinking things need to change but haven't yet found how, or the way, it is all right – you are in the right place to start deciding to make some changes.

▓ Turning things round

Do you find yourself saying things like:

> In the next few months I will start looking for a less stressful job
> When I've finished this project I'll have more time for my friends
> I'll be satisfied when my targets are met
> As soon as I lose weight I'll go to a yoga class.

If this sounds like you, ask yourself what are you really waiting for – identify the reasons why you are reluctant to face your fears or reality. Begin to explore how you might be more proactive, give yourself permission to slow down, give your friends and family some of your time – whatever it is you know you need to do.

OK. First of all, take a few deep breaths in and as you breathe out, relax any tension in your body – really fill your abdomen, chest, neck area and head. Then let go. Let go of the air and as you breathe out let go of all the tension in your feet, legs, abdomen, buttocks, chest, arms, back and neck. Even feel the spaces in your head. Now, imagine yourself looking and feeling as you want to be. Close your eyes and for a few seconds see yourself, life-size, looking, talking, walking, interacting – just the way you want to be. Step into that picture and see from those eyes, hear from those ears and experience how good you feel. Tell yourself:

> I am actively looking for a way to feel less stressed
> I value my friends and seeing them is a priority in my life
> I believe there are more important things in life than making more money
> I do exercise because it makes me fit and healthy.

■ Working out your priorities

It might seem that in order to make progress in finding balance you need to be on full alert, primed to make a decision and to act on it right away. Sometimes, however, unresolved issues require you to take an honest look at what your true priorities really are in order to see that all change needn't involve major shifts – in fact, sometimes by making small changes you can take positive action that will have a big impact on your overall sense of balance. For example:

Recognising that a desire to leave your job may really be an exaggerated reaction to feeling overwhelmed by your overflowing in-tray and having no personal time. Could you make small changes, like consciously scheduling in time to deal with the in-tray, raising the issue of your workload with your employer and also making time to spend with your partner/family/friends?

Acknowledging that you are feeling irritable and stressed and this explains why you are feeling bullied and victimised by someone in your office. The answer might not be to ask to be transferred to another office, but instead to look at the situation honestly and get some help – this could be anything from starting an exercise regime to dealing with your stress levels to assertiveness training to counselling.

Understanding that a desire for an affair may be a way to avoid looking at where you are feeling dissatisfied; what is going wrong in your marriage; perhaps feeling bored with your working life.

■ Taking the time you need

Many major decisions can take a long time to work out; they shift us into a transitional phase. In this phase, the curtains drop so that the stage can be set for a new scene. Sometimes when important decisions need to be made, there is no rush of adrenaline, no sense of excitement; instead of feeling proactive and decisive, it's possible to feel surprisingly blurred and even aimless. There's often the feeling of guilt about wasting time and going around in circular arguments; but the chances are there is a lot going on inside. There might be a lot of inner work you need to do in order to bring about the needed or desired change.

You can relax a bit, because you are doing something – you are cogitating, incubating ideas and working through your feelings and thoughts. You are preparing yourself, finding the resources, making the contacts, setting up the meetings and organising what needs to be put into place so that when the time comes for action, you will be ready.

You may not want to give up parts of your life that you think have worked well enough without your having to give them much attention, for example, a relationship or marriage that seems to work well enough. Then there are the areas that you might not have put energy into recently, for example, an out-dated dream or secret hope of being 'discovered' that you may have become disenchanted with but still cling to. Let it go and start to focus on the present.

■ Move closer to change

Changing careers, partners, or any major part of your life means fundamentally changing yourself. It can mean that you are making a conscious choice to stop doing something that is not utilising your skills and talents, letting go of what might seem like comfort, and taking a chance that you are capable of greater things. It can mean moving to another country where there are challenges as well as great opportunities. It might mean that you are tired of overstretching yourself and want to spend more quality time with your family. It could be let-ting go of your fantasy about someone, your dream about yourself, your belief about others, old relationships, roles and patterns that don't actually work well for you any longer. If something in your life is draining you more than it is giving you energy, stimulation, support, encouragement and nourishment, it is holding you back. Only you know what this might be in your circumstances. Think about this in the context of the following possible work–life balance situations.

Work/Home/Family/Friends: Do you find it harder to neglect your work than to say 'no' to your family? Are you missing out on quality time with your partner/children/friends/ageing parents?

Work/Relationship: Are you tired of being single? Is your relationship under threat because work is dominating your life to such an extent that you haven't made time/space for a partner?

Work/Play: Does your work dominate your life to the extent that you have abandoned hobbies and interests, don't have time to enrol for classes or go away for the weekend or on holiday?

Dreams/Reality: Do you hold a vision of yourself/your future/your situation that is at odds with reality? What are the differences? (Did you envisage yourself in a relationship, as a parent, as a sportsperson, as a homeowner, as living in another country, as travelling, as a performer, as an aid worker?)

Health and Well-being/Low Energy: Are you unfit or unhappy with the state of your health? What are the symptoms? Could they be related to how you care for yourself?

Wealth/Debt: Is your new business idea a high financial risk? Are you constantly struggling to stay afloat financially? Is there another way to look at what you do, how you work, how you spend your money? Is downshifting an option you couldn't afford?

Work/Unemployment: Look at ways you can stay motivated/stay in balance. Use unemployment as an opportunity to take stock of where you are.

Aspirations/Age: Is there a discrepancy between your age and where you expected to be? Do you need to review/plan your goals/recognise that now may be the moment for certain ideas, ambitions, practicalities?

■ The time is now

The time it takes to recognise that an important decision needs to be made can be longer than you might think at the start of the process. A period of anything from six months to three years is usual, but it can take as long as ten years to make a decision about changing a career or lifestyle – by which time the opportunity might have passed and you've missed the moment! Everyone's situation is different; some are more complex than others. Some people need to take time to reflect on what their current position is; they might have incomplete ideas and notions of how they could be different, what they could do, how they've outgrown a job or way of life, how outdated a role seems to be compared with what they feel they want and need to do.

Are you experiencing an uncomfortable period of your life because you want to make changes but don't know where, how or when? Maybe there are so many options you can't decide which one because none strikes you as the main passion or the most feasible route. If this is the case, you need to dig a bit deeper and get closer to what it is you want but don't know anything about – take a step into the unknown and start to give it form and shape. Make a move and try out what possibilities to explore first. You move closer just by noticing how you feel, what you do and what others do. You also get closer by committing to it. This might seem like a big step, but it's true – if you get closer and commit to something that isn't working a) you give it a chance and b) you'll know much sooner if something is going to work because it is in line with your purpose.

Change is going to mean:

> renewing/changing priorities
> rescheduling
> communicating with others
> making allowances for others
> changing your behaviour.

Your old self will be changing as you begin to include your values in how you are living and working, in how you see yourself and others, in how your assumptions and rules for living are shifting. Your old beliefs are being unwound, examined, discarded, replaced, refreshed. This is a slow process and, while you need to be prepared for change, it's also important to be compassionate with yourself as you try out things that might not work straight away, and resilient in keeping on trying something else that moves you to your desired end.

If you are lucky you might be able to negotiate a sabbatical to explore what you want to do – a three-month training course that takes you into the field in which you might like to work, a long summer break in which to take some time for yourself – go on a meditation retreat, or an activity holiday designed to refresh and revitalise like yoga or tai chi. Or if you have a year's redundancy money, you might be able to take the first six months to think, relax and recover before thrusting yourself into outplacement or recruitment or business opportunities.

Everyone needs time to think without phones, emails, TV, conversations. I offer my clients at the end of a four-day course a fifth day of silence. It is a day to quieten, settle and think, a day of incubation and integration. Usually the response from the organisers booking the course is: 'Our people won't like that; they are too busy' – but they love it.

If you have to make a big decision and have been going through anguish, this means you have been taking a serious decision seriously – you are bravely facing up to noticing what needed to be noticed, and are getting ready to break the impasse and make the necessary changes.

■ Transitions – we all go through them

Transitions are often characterised by fallow, unproductive times that can be distracting, confusing, unclear, lacking in information or enough hard evidence to move us forward. Transitions ask for your faith. It helps to be able to access your intuition, your emotional gut reaction as well as your rational sense – no easy matter if they seem to be telling you different things. Maybe you are daring to dream again, to think of how you might live life in a different way, find new ways of working, interact differently, have different friends and spend your time doing different things. You could be in a place where you are lingering between several identities, the outdated one and a half-formed idea of your future one. If this describes your state of mind, you will be feeling the strain of the dissonance and wanting to ease it.

Sometimes someone gives you a different perspective on the matter and points out what might happen if you continue to do nothing, and then a moment will come in which you will see quite decisively what has been happening. But until that moment, while you are in transition, it will help you to acknowledge that you can't skirt around the edges here, or take the lift and bypass the actual situation – you just have to dwell in what might seem like a no-man's land. This might be particularly hard if you are a decisive, impatient achiever used to taking calculated risks, taking control and waving the flag of who you are. In transition, your ego is not in control; it will help you to accept that what is yet to come is in gestation and it requires time to grow the new persona, to develop the right conditions in which to emerge.

■ Every ending is a beginning

Meanwhile, there are probably things you will need to finish off, loose ends to tie up, endings to go through. Endings done well are tough to pull off; there is a tendency to avoid the full experience, to slip out the back door and miss the finale. You need to put as much energy into how to end well as you put into considering alternatives. Being fully present in a process of ending can be demanding but worthwhile. A good ending is defined by your values and ethics, by being kind to yourself and others, being compassionate to yourself and others, by allowing what needs to happen to have some space.

Sometimes the indecision accompanying change can be frustrating and you might feel inclined to rush things. Please be careful at times like this so that you avoid getting into situations you might not be ready for. As you experiment with your new persona you will be putting yourself in situations that could compromise you because you won't be as experienced in this new environment. When starting something new, we all make mistakes. Take care not to get hurt or to hurt others. Sometimes when we have made a big decision we can feel rather cavalier with the exhilaration of it all. Again, it is all about finding balance in each situation. Ask yourself: how can I be who I am while experimenting with this new me? If you encounter difficulties, find someone you can trust to talk it through. If you encounter a difficulty with someone, it usually helps to try to clear it up straight away instead of leaving it unresolved.

Sometimes in periods of transition we are asked to deal with difficulties that test our maturity and readiness to move on. For example, have been pulled up, criticised, given a bit of a telling-off or some harsh feedback? If so, try to calm down and look at the situation, notice your responses and be aware of how they might reflect a pattern or point to a lesson that needs to be learned. Ask yourself: 'What sort of person do I want to become? Do I like myself? Will I like myself if I do that? Would the person I most respect and admire, respect and admire me for doing this?' The outcome might be important, but so is how you deal with the situation. Learning from experience is what really matters, not coming out on top or being seen to win. This is an important life skill to develop.

Develop essential skills and resources

Chapter 5
Life skills and strategies

- ❏ Find your inner strength
- ❏ Take a balanced view
- ❏ Become more resourceful
- ❏ Cultivate a positive attitude

Earlier we looked at how we need to review and renew outdated attitudes and our life rules. The next step is to learn, develop and practise life skills as essential resources that can help you actively work towards creating the work–life balance that suits you. These life skills and strategies will increase your state of well-being, and enable you to feel more in control and better able to deal with unexpected challenges and obstacles. They will give you the resources you need to work through stressful or difficult situations and come out feeling that you have behaved according to your values. We all have untapped reservoirs of inner strength that we can express through these qualities – it just takes some practice, and you will find your search for balance begins to open up much more as you develop these skills.

■ Courage

Courage is a vital skill in breaking negative cycles and making decisions. It is a practical, everyday skill that you can practise when you need to take action that will result in a better situation and some kind of resolution that enables you and others to feel better. Most of us feel hesitant and fearful at times – this is natural and not a sign of weakness – and you can start with something very small, like sending back a cup of cold coffee in a restaurant, to begin to believe in your courage.

Start with some small challenge and watch how this skill develops. Putting courage into practice can mean, for example, taking a stand on issues that go against 'public opinion' but you think are moral; perhaps taking what you believe to be a correct and humane attitude when others are giving way to prejudice; doing your best in the face of difficulty, an obstacle or an ordeal.

In what situations have you displayed courage in the past? List them, and include all the times you surprised yourself. You'll need a pen and paper for this. Go for twenty, no matter how trivial they seem to you. Write them all down, in as much detail as you like.

Now look at your list. Do you need at the moment to take specific action in order to find/access your courage – for example, is there a situation that you need to deal with, a person you need to talk to; do you need to attend assertiveness training, a self-defence class, a public-speaking course? Where could you do with more courage in your life right now?

■ Perspective

Having, gaining and maintaining a sense of perspective over time is crucial in helping you through whatever you are experiencing. No matter what is going on in your work or life, there is no one way to view the situation you find yourself in. You can deal with it, whatever it is, by shifting your perspective a little.

Breathe and relax. Think of someone you like and admire, maybe a hero of yours, maybe a passed-away relative, your best friend or a dear mentor. Imagine them in front of you, step into their picture and see from their eyes your situation, hear what they are saying and how they are saying it. Usually perspective allows us to understand, be empathic, see the good and the bad without judgement, adjust, adapt or leave it alone, yet send compassion.

You have a perspective if you can extract yourself from the present and take a view over time; if you learn from the past and can imagine the future. You also show perspective if you can be empathic and see things from another's point of view. If you regularly see your friends, mix with a wide range of people and take a broad view of what is happening around you, this will increase your perspective and give you a more balanced view.

Having a balanced time perspective has been found to be an essential psychological resource that will stand you in good stead in difficult times.

The focus and perspective you put on your situation will radically alter your feelings about it, and make it easier to maintain a sense of equanimity. As the saying goes – and experience confirms its truth – if you change the way you see the world, what you see will change.

Are you giving quality focus to everything you do at the moment, one thing at a time? Are you being creative in the way you view the situation, from different viewpoints over time and taking into account other people's perspectives?

Think of the thing that is troubling you:

Now think of it as if two years have passed. How are you thinking about it now? How do you feel about it now?

Think of yourself as a child and have this child look at you grappling with your situation. Ask the child what it thinks and feels. How has your perspective changed now?

■ Optimism and positivity

Optimism is a huge factor in whether someone finds satisfaction in life. Optimistic people expect, look for and work for the best in moving towards the future; they see the positive and the humorous aspects in most situations and are able to work through difficult times more easily than people who tend to focus on the negative aspects of change instead of the opportunities.

Some people are born optimistic, but it is also a skill that you can learn and put into practice – for example, earlier we looked at how reframing will help you cultivate an optimistic and positive attitude, so use the exercises there to increase this quality and put you into a positive state of mind.

Think about what you have achieved so far, and remember the skills and the resources you have accumulated during your life. By appreciating your strengths, what you overcame, the positive outcomes from the past, you can bring optimism about yourself and your capabilities into the present and the future.

Question: Do you see the glass as half full or half empty? Do you find it easier to focus on what isn't right than what is? Do you need to start to work on reframing some of your perceptions in order to enjoy your life and help others around you enjoy theirs?

Apart from a few really difficult things in life, like the death of a child or loved one, you can often find positives in any situation. Dig deep. What is facing you right now that is helping you grow, helping you discover, that is positive?

■ Emotional intelligence and skills

Recently a lot of work has been done to understand the impact of what is now called emotional intelligence, a term popularised by Daniel Goleman in the 1990s. Fundamentally, emotional intelligence involves being self-aware, managing your moods and having the interpersonal flexibility to engage with a wide variety of people and their different states of mind.

If you have well-developed emotional intelligence you will understand yourself well and be comfortable naming your strengths and weaknesses. You will be able consciously to choose your behaviour, and you are good at reading and influencing the moods of others. Anyone who works or lives with others uses emotional intelligence in successful relating, communicating and interacting.

Emotional and social skills are critically important in finding fulfilment, and an essential resource in negotiating work–life balance. Social skills and empathy can also be included in the broad term emotional intelligence. The ability to communicate and interact with others successfully is essential not only in times of change, but in life generally.

Spending some time cultivating this important skill will help you in:

Building your trustworthiness and creating respectful relationships
Developing a wider repertoire of communication abilities
Understanding that the perception others have of you matters and that
    you have to manage that perception and impact
Working for the good of others as well as yourself

Do you avoid getting up close and personal with people around you? How comfortable are you with intimacy, exploring, talking about and showing your feelings? How prepared are you to put in effort to talk about, work on and develop your relationship skills? Are you getting out enough? Do you need to widen the range of people you mix with? (For example, if you are an accountant and mix only with your colleagues, it might be worth trying something completely different: take up aikido or volunteer to do some outdoors conservation work, say.)

Write a letter to someone who has been a major positive influence in your life. Write to thank them, using as much descriptive language as possible, and tell them about the effect they had on you.

Schedule in some time of solitude in which to have a quiet think about things. Then schedule in and organise an extra engagement – meet up with an old friend or initiate meeting a new person or group. Do both in the same week and notice what the fulfilment of that balance does for you.

▦ Faith and hope

You have to take risks sometimes. No one is ever completely ready – it sometimes needs a leap of faith. Faith is about using your strengths as virtues; in the service of something larger and more lasting than you are. If you are someone who has faith, you might describe yourself as a religious or a spiritual person. Perhaps you are someone who enjoys discussing your particular philosophy in life; perhaps you feel connected to something bigger than yourself and believe in a higher purpose that serves the good of the universe. Some people have faith just in themselves, in their own abilities to succeed. Wherever you find your faith and hope, it is an essential quality that really helps when times are hard, when decisions need to be made or when you are facing up to big life issues that involve loss.

Are you still living in the past? How open and flexible is your mind? Are you holding on to a dream, a way of life, a role that is blocking progress? Are you thinking enough about alternative possibilities? Do you have new dreams and believe that there can be pathways to those goals? Can you become motivated to use those pathways? Are you living your faith?

■ Your attitude towards work

I have often heard people say jokingly: 'Nobody ever said on their deathbed that they wished they'd spent more time in the office.' In times when work–life balance is in question, this might seem to be a reasonable assertion. Some people, however, spend long hours at work but do not really focus on giving their best, and as a result go home feeling tired and apathetic. While you are at work, try out the strategy of being there more consciously and making a contribution. You might be surprised at how things change.

If you are fortunate enough to like or even love the work you do, you will recognise how lucky you are. If you are happy in other areas of your life, you might be someone who does the work others would dislike – life is all about balance. Finding balance will help you to keep focused, diligent and able to work with a good spirit, whatever your job might be.

Do you have important goals at work? Have you achieved them and wonder what to do next? Haven't you dared/bothered to have them? Are they beating you? Are you stuck in old-fashioned, negative views like: 'I work just to pay the bills'? What is your idea of success? Can you say where you find success in your life and work?

Think back to your last working day – how could you have been if you had put your best foot forward, if you had given all of your being, the best of yourself? Think through the next working day you have and plan and visualise giving the best of yourself. Commit to it.

Ask yourself, 'If I could change one thing about myself that would make a real difference to my working life, what would it be?' Maybe do one for home life and one for work life. You may need to review and reset yourself one goal – make it bold, but feasible. Time-frame it, work out the steps you need to take to achieve. Write all this down and put it where you can see it.

Honesty

Another old saying that happens to be true, usually, is 'honesty is the best policy'.

You tell the truth and you tell the whole truth, you are genuine and present yourself as you really are; you are truthful to yourself and true to yourself. But how honest are you with yourself, in your relationships, in how you feel about the people you work with – it's so easy to avoid in ourselves what we see as negative or dislike in others. It can be difficult to see things as they really are if you prefer to go by your own version of what's happening. Again, go back to your little life rules and consider where your assumptions, prejudices, patterns, habits, might be getting in the way of honesty.

Are you hiding from being honest with yourself because you can't seem to find the time or the space or the resources to deal with what you might find? Are you not being honest with others for fear of repercussions, for not wanting to hurt them, for fear of conflict or change? Who aren't you communicating with or talking to openly?

Think of someone you are not comfortable with at the moment, and how this is affecting your progress in finding work–life balance. How can you get to the next level of honesty with this person? What will be your first step? Make it.

Perseverance and commitment

If you have the qualities of perseverance and commitment you don't give up readily and generally finish what you start. You are reliable, you do what you say you will do and often more. You are fully engaged and committed rather than just involved. These are useful life skills to cultivate, especially when you are setting out on a new venture; trying to set up your own business; in fact any shift or change will require you to commit your energy and time into making it work.

What have you given up on? Can you remobilise your intentions, energy and effort? Where do you need to put focus, energy and effort?

What do you miss? What did it give you? Think of something that could have done with a bit more perseverance from you. How could you recreate that opportunity or get back those feelings doing what you did? If you are at a cross-roads, commit more, move closer. This might seem to be counter-intuitive but if you go ahead and do it you will certainly know more quickly whether or not you have chosen the right path.

■ Compassion

Taking care of yourself and giving attention to your needs is the beginning of finding balance. Usually we see compassion as something we have for others, but if you really care for yourself, you will know that you also need to be compassionate towards yourself in order to succeed in what you want to do.

Compassion is essential if you are prepared to face up to reality. If you are holding onto something that doesn't seem to be working, or hasn't worked, it could mean simply that it isn't going to work. Sometimes with the best of intentions and effort, a situation remains stuck, or doesn't work out because of lack of resources or wrong conditions.

Sometimes we need to know when to let go and rebuild, reframe, find another plan or way forward. In a situation like this compassion for yourself is essential in order to let go and make space for renewal; to forgive yourself and anyone else who might be involved, to give yourself permission to improvise for a while until you are back on track. Compassion will help you turn towards a new direction, be kind to yourself about your own mistakes; the energy of compassion will encourage you to release outdated dreams, ideas, plans, visions, relationships, blocks and patterns of behaviour that no longer work for you.

Take a deep breath in, expand your abdomen. Fill your abdomen, your lungs, chest and neck with air and relax all tensions as you exhale. Do it again – deep breathe in, fully into the abdomen, through the chest to the neck and into your head and as you breathe out, let go.

Now, ask yourself:

What do I need to forgive myself for?
What do I need to let go of?
What do I need to forgive in others?

■ Practical intelligence

Common sense and good problem-solving capability are great life skills to have that can make a real difference in how successful you are in achieving your goals. You have practical intelligence if you examine your heart and your mind before making a decision, and if you are enthusiastic and resourceful in solving problems. Another example of practical intelligence is political astuteness – being aware of people's agendas, perspective and viewpoints. Having good judgement involves tapping into your inner wisdom and listening to others.

Make a pledge that for the rest of today you are going to do two things: be patient and be focused. Engage fully, mindfully, in everything you do, focusing on one thing at a time – giving it total quality time. Engage with who you need to in order to have the space to concentrate. If you are interrupted, relax, be patient. Notice how much easier things go, how much you get done, how calmer life seems.

In your preparation, do a little visualisation. This might seem to you a long way from practical intelligence, but it will help you feel calm, patient and focused if you have difficulty getting into that state of mind. Imagine a beautiful place in a natural country setting, maybe somewhere you once visited. See the whole panoramic view, feel the breeze and the sun on your body, smell nature's smells around you and hear the sounds. In this wonderful place you see some-one who looks radiantly content and wise as if they have lived thousands of years without ageing. As you look closer you see it is you – the real you, the essence of you, without any role or mask. This is the wise you, the beautiful you and you fall in love with this person. What do you see about this person, what are their qualities? What do they think about your life as it is at the moment? What are they telling you? What are they telling you about your resources, your strengths, your way out of this situation?

■ Managing mood and motivation

Managing your moods is a fundamental part of maturity and a predictor of whether you will live well as you age. If you wish to influence people you live and work with this will be much easier if first you learn the skills involved in managing yourself. In the corporate world, leaders are being assessed for their high emotional intelligence because EQ, as it is called, has a real and long-lasting effect on bottom-line results, sometimes doubling and even tripling productivity. In one study of American insurance companies, the most successful (judged by growth and results) all had one differentiating critical factor: the senior teams had the ability to create a positive climate through the management of their moods and emotions. Your perception of things is radically altered by your mood. Any projective test, such as seeing pictures in different ways, will show that you see what your mind wants to see, and what you see is largely a representation of what you are feeling.

These concepts theorise about what can be known already from experience – for example, if you are upset, you will not be able to engage well with others, and as anyone who has experienced distress will confirm, it impairs your ability to read situations and others accurately. You can transmit moods around the house and your workplace without saying a thing! It has been said that even strangers can transmit a mood to other people – while keeping a passive body posture and facial expression and without saying a word. If there is anger, irritation and despondency among colleagues working in the same office, it affects everyone to varying degrees.

Anyone who wants to influence people around them could learn a useful skill by cultivating an awareness of how their emotional style has an impact on others. The basis of emotional intelligence is knowing yourself, cultivating self-awareness. Your self-awareness is already increasing as you are working your way through this book.

Part of emotional intelligence is about self-regulation, or how you discipline yourself to reframe situations, use your strengths and values to help control or redirect unhelpful impulses, moods and habits. Keeping up your motivation is crucial to generate a positive mood and climate in others.

Where do you find inspiration?
Who do you find inspiring?
When and who last inspired you?
(Let them know!)
What places do you find uplifting?
Refreshing?
Calming?
Inspiring?

How can you engineer it so that you are in the company and surrounded
by the things that nourish you?

Where?

With whom?

When?

Managing your emotions

The way you talk to yourself when you are at a crossroads, in a difficult situation
or a crisis is the key to how you will emerge at the other end of the process, and
how long it will take to complete. The AMULET coping process (an amulet being
a charm worn to give protection) is a useful resource that you can use at any
time to train yourself in an effective technique that will help you acknowledge a
situation and work it through to its resolution. Think it through in the context of
a past situation to see how it can help you achieve a sense of clarity and
completion.

There are six steps in the AMULET process of self-talk:

1 **A**ccept what has happened
2 **M**ove on to rational thinking
3 **U**se reframe to extract something positive out of the situation
4 **L**isten deeply to what it is about the situation you are facing
    that is really upsetting you
5 **E**ncourage yourself to be compassionate
6 **T**ake some time out to do something pleasant.

Step 1: Accept what has happened

Give yourself permission to feel what you are feeling. Trying to stop yourself
feeling bad, pushing something under the carpet, distracting yourself too soon,
blocking it out of your mind or thinking you can control it might seem to be a
good way to stop yourself feeling upset, but this is rarely effective in the long
term. It is better just to acknowledge what you feel – 'OK, this is terrible. It has
happened. It is normal to feel bad. It would be abnormal not to feel awful.'

Step 2: Move on to rational thinking

From time to time we have all responded to something and then later found out we made a mistaken assumption, and the trouble caused was actually our fault. Similarly, have you ever been confronted with a problem and felt surprised by how you reacted? A useful skill to practise is the technique of 'listening and calming self-talk'. This will identify what you say to yourself in situations like this, and you can then use calming self-talk to influence your feelings and actions more positively. Think of times when you have overreacted or reacted too quickly – were you being rational or exaggerating, or filling in the spaces with your own story and anxieties? Listen to what pushes your buttons and work with that.

Calming self-talk simply means firstly that you tell yourself to stay calm, to take a deep breath or two or three, to relax, to take it easy, to focus. Then you tell yourself how you can cope using simple, true statements like 'I coped with X so I can cope with this' or self-affirming statements like 'I can do this'. It may be helpful to think what you would like to do, intend to do, must do. This is where you need to gather yourself and use a bit of self-discipline to regain enough composure to think rationally, realistically and constructively.

Ask yourself:

What is the worst-case scenario?

How likely is that?

Is the evidence a bit thin on the ground – could it be you're exaggerating?

What more do you need to find out?

Who has been in a similar situation that could help you?

Are you imagining the worst?

How else could things turn out?

Step 3: Use reframe to extract something positive

This may take some time if you are going through a trauma, in which case you may well be in shock. In the early stages of a traumatic event the initial shock is best dealt with by focusing on your immediate well-being and safety instead of starting to deal with what has happened. People who have had a big shock often say, 'I just can't believe it.' The mind has switched off for a while; it is 'playing dead' until it feels more able to cope. The important thing is not to let this stage linger but to get professional help if you need it in order gradually to acknowledge the reality of what has happened.

Once you have come out of the haze of disbelief, it is important to find something, however superficial it might seem at first, that can be reframed in a positive way about the situation. In time, the learning may be deeper and greater.

For example, you could tell yourself:

Even though I would never have wanted this, it is teaching me to … and I am learning an important lesson from what happened.

Ask yourself what a mentor or wise friend would think about this, and what they might say to you. You can use this technique to help you get out of tunnel vision in many different situations.

Take some time to think clearly and find the best way of dealing with the situation by seeing what constructive things you can do right now to improve it as much as possible. Concentrate actively on whatever positive features of the situation you can create, but be careful not to generate a false or unrealistic illusion. It is possible to keep a positive mental attitude if you really concentrate, stay focused and have the support you need.

Step 4: Listen deeply to yourself

Take some time to ask yourself what it is about the situation you are facing that is really upsetting you. If your reaction seems a little disproportional to what is happening, this could be because someone has broken one of your 'rules', or crossed one of your values or beliefs about how things should be.

Sometimes these beliefs interfere with your ability to live the life you want and they can often explain why we overreact to something or just can't make an important decision (this might also be the result of conflicting beliefs vying for attention). Use helpful 'self-talk' by specifying your goal, and break down the task into small steps. Focus on the moment of taking the first step, and then the next. One step at a time. Remember that your fears are often F.E.A.R. – False Evidence Appearing Real.

Step 5: Encourage yourself to be compassionate

Be as compassionate to yourself and others as you can. Sometimes when something happens it is an automatic response to blame yourself first, and while everyone has to take responsibility for what they do, this isn't the same as taking the blame.

Encourage yourself to be compassionate:

> Use helpful self-talk as if you were talking to your dearest best friend
> Be kind to yourself!

On the other hand, some people are always ready to jump to conclusions and blame others first. Again, it is helpful to think about responsibility. Blaming others is often an easy option but it can reinforce the tendency to make assumptions and judgements, and eventually undermines your resilience. Try instead to develop compassion for others. If you stop asking why and just accept there is nothing you can do for the time being, you will avoid being stuck in a negative cycle. If you blame yourself, you could be over-personalising. No matter how difficult or complex the situation might be, a small change in your attitude or behaviour can have a profound and far-reaching effect on you, as well as on others.

Step 6: Take some time to do something pleasant

Avoid spending too much time re-running an event or situation. After you have done what you can, try to do something pleasant to give yourself a break and shift your energy. Engaging in a distraction will clear the air and give you some space to see things in a different light. Diverting your thoughts to something positive is a useful skill to learn. Tell yourself: there is nothing productive that I can do right now to help and nothing to be gained by worsening how I feel. I am going to help myself by doing X which will distract me, help my mood and put me in a better state of mind to deal with things later.

Finally, use affirmations that focus on what you have achieved and how good you feel about that. Maximise your chance of success and fulfilment by bringing to mind what you have worked through, what you achieved, how you emerged a better and wiser person.

■ Trust

An important part of self-management is trust. Trust is an essential component of healthy relationships and is relevant to work–life balance because first you have to trust in your own ability, and at some point you need to trust others. If you employ or supervise others, they will give their best if they feel that they are trusted to do a good job. If you are looking to achieve more work–life balance and want to ask your boss about flexible working, for example, you will need to show that you can still be trusted to show commitment to your work and to the organisation.

Who respects and trusts you?
Do people around you tell you about their heartfelt goals?

Who doesn't trust you, do you think, and why?
Who do you not trust and why?
Do you suspect the people around you of hidden agendas?
Do you not trust them to be honest and reliable?
How does this relate to your little life rules and your values?

Trust is built on making yourself vulnerable. How vulnerable are you prepared to make yourself? Where you lack trust, it is probably because you fear being betrayed or are doing everything you can to avoid being betrayed or disappointed (again). You can't have trust or give trust unless you are:

a) comfortable with yourself
b) trust yourself
c) have agreed with others an ethical framework.

Ask yourself what conversations could you be having that you aren't. Ask yourself what you could be doing and being that allows people to trust you more.

Everyone wants to be respected and trusted yet most of us respect and trust only a few people we are close to in our work and personal lives. The conditions under which trust is generated are those in which both individual and mutual pay-offs are explicit – yet how often do we engage in such a straightforward way? Think about what overall goals and parts of goals are shared by you and others in your working and personal relationships. In any organisation, business or relationship, trust is something you need to develop in order to move towards a situation where everyone is happy and feels that their wishes and gifts are being respected.

■ Considering others

As you make changes in your life, other people will be affected. They have an invested interest in you. Sometimes that interest is in wanting you to stay the same, sometimes it is changing you to be the way they want you to be for them, sometimes it is about changing in the way you want to. Pull together what you have learned so far about yourself.

> Who have you been?
> Who are you now?
> Who do you want to be?

Think about the people in your life – family, partners, friends, boss, colleagues, clients, children, neighbours, club associates. Draw a map of how they connect to you. Try putting yourself in their shoes, see from their eyes how you are going to change and what you need changing around you. Be aware of who will support you and who will resist, and consider how you will approach this situation.

Based on the work of psychologist Dr Janet Reibstein, the following Give–Get model is an easy way for you to remember and focus on what makes a happy relationship, analyse what is working and what needs attention, and learn tips that can make a difference to your relationships.

> **G**ratitude: take time to say what you appreciate about the other
> **I**nvite changes: say what you need/where you need help
> **V**alues: you need to be aware of your and their values and principles
> **E**njoy each other's strengths and differences. Appreciate the diversity.

> **G**enerosity breeds generosity: it's about the mutuality of relationships
> **E**nable by showing loyalty, protect them, be trustworthy
> **T**ime: make time for them where you give focused attention.

What does this tell you about the state of your relationships with key people you need to bring along with you? When was the last time you showed your appreciation for them? Did they get it? What would they 'get'?

Are you doing well at 'inviting changes'? Have you taken the courage to tell someone how you are feeling, what you are thinking, what you need?

You know your values now. Do you think they would be able to guess them by how you have been behaving?

What do you think they would assume were yours? Do you know theirs? Are you assuming?

When was the last time you truly enjoyed each other's best side? How could you replicate those surroundings, that time, that context?

What did you last make explicit, loud and clear, unambiguous, the mutuality in the relationship?

What conversations could you have that would make explicit your co-dependence and the mutual payback of actions?

Were they in your trust circle?

Were you in theirs?

What more could you be doing to show your loyalty?

What more could you do to test or invite their trustworthiness?

How could you look after them, protect them, a little better?

What is the quality of your attention when you see them?

What could you do to make space for them to let them know you value them in your life?

If you are in transition, be aware of any tendency to isolate yourself. Isolation makes it difficult to ask for what you need, and the danger is that the other party feels less connected and less obligated to us as well. The loss of a give-and-get connection breaks down the sense of mutuality, and when you emphasise give and get, a real sense of co-dependence stirs and people rise up to support – even protect – each other.

Before you try to influence someone, make sure the relationship is good. To improve key relationships before you can negotiate anything, remember that it helps to try to understand first instead of trying to be understood. Before starting negotiations, make an effort to understand the other person's perspective, needs, wants. There's something you can do to help you in this. Get a pen.

Now write down all the words that come into your head when you say the word 'understand'.

Note the range of responses. If you ask someone else to do this and compare their answers with yours, you will see that even the concept of understanding is complex.

■ The art of listening

Understanding something from someone else's point of view is a complex, demanding activity. It usually involves good listening and observation skills. Listening demands the character to hold the tension, hold back from interrupting, reacting or solving. It requires humility – you need to adopt an attitude of not knowing. Be so open that you really listen to their every word, listen to every pitch and tone change. Observe the speaker's body language, not to make judgements but so that you can enter their world for a little while. Don't fall into the trap of thinking that everyone wants an opinion or an answer. Don't try to teach but find out what it is you are learning. Listening requires trust and respect – the more open you are to trust and respect others, the more likely you will enter their perspective long enough to understand.

If you take some time to review and cultivate these essential life skills, the chances are other people will be more willing to support you when it comes to making changes that will improve your work–life balance.

Having a vision
will inspire you
to action

Chapter 6
Creating vision and direction

❏ Prepare to take a new direction

❏ Create your mission statement

❏ Evaluate your assets, strengths and qualities

❏ Merge with deep life interests

This is an important turning point in the book and in your work–life balance project. Your willingness to create a vision and vision statement is akin to your belief in your potential and this is the time to make a bold move. It is tantamount to making a declaration.

The founder of Sony, for example, started with a prospectus of principles by which he wanted to do business in something for someone. When you create a living document of who you are, it is a powerful message that says you are in charge of yourself, you are taking responsibility and are in control of the levers that guide your mood and behaviour.

Let's take a look at how you would like things to be different. Once we get into our teens, people usually stop asking us what we want to be or do. Asking questions will help you to continue dreaming and envisioning a better future. Having a vision will help you in getting to where you really want to be. However modest it may be, having a vision is the starting point in achieving balance and fulfilment in your work and life. Your vision is linked to your soul; it should be uplifting and compel you towards a future you consider to be worthwhile. It's your depiction of your desired future situation. It's perfectly OK if it seems a little unrealistic from where you are now – having a vision will inspire you to action.

When you write your own goals and expectations you make a decision about your future, which gives you clarity, intensity of purpose, motivation, direction, positivity and energy for yourself and others. The following exercise will give you a good foundation for taking whatever action is needed.

Step 1: In the space opposite, write down in column A all the things you would like to do in the next fifteen years. Make the list as long as you like; get an extra sheet of paper if you don't have enough room here. Looking at the list, focus your attention on this life. Imagine you are leading this life – a life that you are really passionate about and would love to have.

Step 2: Fill in column B *as if you were already doing these things*. Write affirmative statements about yourself in the present tense. For instance, if you want to branch out on your own and move out of the city, write something like; 'I have more energy, feel less stressed and am much more productive now that I'm working for myself.' If you are single and want a partnership, write: 'I feel fulfilled now that I spend less time at work and more time with someone special.'

If you want to spend less time at work and more time at home, write: 'I am enjoying the relaxation of playing cards with the family one evening.'

Step 3: Now imagine yourself doing all of those things. Really see yourself in this new role – how you look, how you dress, how you sound, how others are responding to you, how you feel.

Step 4: Step into that you, and ask: Is this what I really wanted? Is there anything else I need or want? Record the answer and build it into your scene.

Step 5: Check out the reality and how feasible it all is. Identify anything you might need to amend.

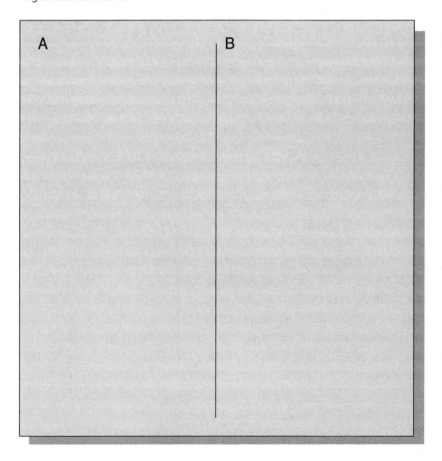

■ Putting it into practice

Fundamentally, finding balance and fulfilment in a role, career or environment that you will engage with and be able to get into flow with depends on how you merge the following:

1 Your vision – a sense of where you belong
2 Your mission – a sense of your purpose, why you are here
3 Your values – what principles you want to live by and what will satisfy
4 Your assets – your strengths, what makes you feel competent
5 Your life interests – what will enable you to engage, keep motivated

Your mission represents your fundamental reasons for existing beyond just making money. To earn a living used to be the means by which we were able to have an interesting life – now, work itself can become interesting, and if we create how we work, it can be a way of self-expression. Naming your mission is like developing your self-concept. For some it might be a calling or a true vocation to which you want to devote your time, energy and skills; but it doesn't have to be a great quest for achievement either at work or in leisure. Your mission might be to give to the world your kindness, compassion, humour, honesty. The following questions will help you think about and focus on your mission.

If you didn't need to earn a living and the world stayed the same whether you were earning or not, your home was secure, your family and friends were looked after, would you be happy to live and work in the same way, to have the same future? Think about what work you would do in that situation, and why.

What work would you do if you had unlimited wealth?
If you stopped work, what would you miss?
What do you love so much that you'd pay to do it? What do you feel really passionate about?
How do you really feel about money, how important is it to you and what else is as or more important?
What would be unlived if your life had ended yesterday?
What dreams, what talents, what ideas would have been left unlived?
What fascinates you?
What body of knowledge consistently attracts you?

You are at a turning point. The next phase of your life is taking shape now as you enter a deeper level of honesty with yourself. This is an appropriate time to learn something you've wanted to do better or differently. You may wish to be someone different. Reflect on how you would like to create your work–life balance; what you would like to achieve that would improve your quality of life. This is your opportunity to begin the unlived you, the unrealised you.

▪ Create your vision

Someone once said, 'You are only powerful on that for which you make a stand.' Yet it matters not what role you have but what you contribute. Take care not to get stuck in the decision of your role. It's important not to get limited by the wording of that contract because that will restrict your growth, development and fulfilment. Organisations that succeed are innovative and sometimes this means joining in to make something come alive – it means being prepared to be spontaneous, generous and engaging in the action in order to be part of and create the whole.

Maybe you had a vision, a fantasy, a daydream, a wish for yourself when you were a child about how you would like your life to be when you grew up. Perhaps you kept that dream for a while before developing more practical ideas about yourself. People who have achieved noted success succeeded in keeping their vision or created new ones. They usually have a vision of themselves. Whether they talk about it or share it with anyone depends on their level of discretion, but they have one and they think of it daily.

What visions, dreams, fantasies, expectations, hopes of yourself did you have that you had to let go of? What are the qualities of those visions? Identify what attracted you to the vision.

The vision
For example: High-level executive working in New York with lots of
*   boyfriends*

Qualities
International environment, high pay, exciting work, freedom in
*   relationships*

Spend a few moments appreciating your achievements so far. Acknowledge your strengths, your efforts and your qualities.

Think back to the things you have achieved that you feel good about. They might be large or small, and they have to be meaningful to you. Write them in the space below, and what qualities you showed to achieve them. Once you've got the ball rolling, you'll need an extra sheet of paper!

For example, from the ages of 4–14: *Won the hurdle race.* Qualities and resources used: *Overcoming shyness about being overweight, determination (because not a natural talent), effort.*

Things I have achieved
From the ages of 4–14 Qualities and resources used

From the ages of 15–24 Qualities and resources used

From the ages of 25–34 Qualities and resources used

From the age of 35+ Qualities and resources used

Often the things that we are really good at we hardly consider to be a talent – maybe we have had so much good feedback on them in the past that it sounds like a record playing, or perhaps it feels so natural to us that we shrug off compliments. One of the best ways to lead a successful life is not to beat ourselves up for what we aren't that good at, but to use the things we are good at. Let's take a look at the skills you have acquired along your life.

> Are you settled or at a crossroads right now? Why are you at a cross-roads? What have you learnt to do in terms of what you consider to be your role? How did you learn those things?
>
> Thinking of your challenge – are there alternative ways of going about things? Which ones are you actively exploring? How?
>
> Who has been helpful or inspiring for you and your thought process? Who hasn't been helpful?
>
> How would you describe this period? What has been the hardest? Where have you been really pleased with yourself?
>
> In your last job, what did you learn to do well? Why did you leave? Think about the transition period. Who made a difference and why? How many different kinds of ideas or possibilities did you consider? How far did you go with each? What was the hardest thing about the whole process? What came more easily than you expected it to?
>
> What about the job before last? What did you learn to do in terms of leadership or yourself from that job? Why did you leave? Identify the changes you had to make as a person in development. What worked as a learning method – was it someone, a book, a course – what?
>
> What was the hardest thing about the whole process? What did you surprise yourself about? What did you learn about yourself at that time of your life? What were the ups from that job? What were the downs?
>
> Where did you make your best contribution? Why is that, do you think?

▦ Create a SWOT Analysis

It's time now to bring all this work up to date and create a realistic picture of the options that are available to you. A SWOT analysis identifies your Strengths, Weaknesses, Opportunities and Threats, and enables you to examine each option you might be considering in these terms.

The ability to be realistic about your weaknesses is a very useful resource. A weakness can be something you just need to give some attention to; you might benefit from picking up some knowledge about a particular topic, or maybe there is a skill that you haven't practised for a while. Sometimes you may need to delve a little deeper to become familiar with your 'demons' – your inner obstacles, fears and inhibitors.

When you begin to think about your strengths, include what you appreciate about yourself. Include everything you can think of: a sense of humour, tenacity or resilience, the ability to map-read or grow organic vegetables, good communication skills or the ability to get on with a wide range of people. When you feel good, your mental effectiveness and efficiency goes up, you become more flexible in your thinking, more able to understand complex information and better at making judgements that take your values into account.

Here are some questions that might help you in this exercise.

Strengths

What will help you achieve your goals? What skills do you have? Can you market your reputation? Do you have a winning attitude? Are you tenacious? Do you have a good support network? Can you foster self-belief under pressure?

Weaknesses

What is preventing you from living the life you aspire to? This is not necessarily about material wealth or status, it may mean gaining time to be with or make friends and get closer to your family or partner. Consider the financial realities: can you afford to downshift? On balance are long, high-stress hours on high pay better at this stage than long, low-stress hours on low pay? Is more time a reality or a pipe dream?

Opportunities

Make a list of all your resources and constraints – turn them around to make them positive. Cost your dream. Put the facts and figures on a spreadsheet.

Threats

What is likely to get in the way of your achieving your goal? Outside factors, lack of funds, low drive or self-motivation?

■ Merge your assets with life interests

Look at your strengths and name the top five. Make sure they are the ones you like using and can see yourself enjoying giving more of and for longer.

Now we look at how your life interests can be merged with your assets. Deeply embedded life interests are not meant to be hobbies, like fly-fishing or skiing. They are not topics you have had a life-long interest in, such as birds or war poetry – these things rarely can be turned into a career. Instead, look at your passions that have lasted over time and which fit your personality. How do your strengths relate to what satisfies you? Here are some categories of deeply embedded life interests:

Technology
    Aspects: How things work. Machines and processes
    Types of work: Engineering computing, technical specialisms
Quantitative analysis
    Aspects: Dealing with numbers, forecasting, modelling
    Types of work: Accounting, research, data
Conceptual
    Aspects: Abstract thinking
    Types of work: Academia
Creative product development
    Aspects: Creative arts, literature, starting new ventures
    Types of work: Writing, graphic art, new business ideas
Education, welfare, health, development
    Aspects: Helping people
    Types of work: Teaching, medicine, psychotherapy, coaching, counselling
Managing people
    Aspects: Day-to-day basics of helping people achieve goals
    Types of work: Management
Influencing and ideas
    Aspects: Negotiating, influencing, telling stories
    Types of work: Training, PR, international relations
Business control
    Aspects: Making decisions, accountability
    Types of work: Running a business

■ Get in touch with your future

Imagine it is your 80th birthday party and you are doing well. Imagine how you would look as a wiser, respected person. One of your oldest friends comes over with a photograph diary and you look through the presentation of your life – the positives and negatives, the conflicts and dilemmas.

Who do you see there and who do you want to be there?

What do you want them to say about you?

What are you going to say about your life?

When did you find out what you needed as opposed to what everyone else wanted you to do?

What really made you laugh?

When did you have the most fun?

Who were your best friends in the end?

When did you feel great?

How did you get out of what you didn't want to do?

When you got what you wanted or needed, what did you do to initiate that?

What were you a force for in the world?

What would you want on your epitaph?

What is your big, bold, wild wish?

And what makes you feel you can't do it?

I can't, as one of my colleagues says, is I-can-engage-in-the-act-of-not-doing. It is an excuse, a choice: it will help you to recognise this and decide if it's the choice you want to be making. Remember this quote when you feel you can't do something:

A new idea is first condemned as ridiculous and then dismissed as trivial until it finally becomes what everybody knows.   *William James, 1842–1910*

BE BOLD. Write your epitaph.

....

....

....

William Pitt Junior has this epitaph on him in the Guildhall, Great Hall, London:

> For these high purposes, he was gifted by divine providence
>
> Endowments, rare in their separate excellence
>
> Wonderful in their combination
>
> Judgment, imagination, memory, wit, force and acuteness of reasoning
>
> Eloquence, copious and accurate, commanding and persuasive
>
> And suited from its splendour to the dignity of his mind
>
> And to the authority of his station
>
> A lofty spirit, a mild and ingenious temper
>
> Warm and steadfast in friendship, towards enemies he was forbearing and forgiving
>
> His industry was not relaxed by confidence in his great abilities; his indulgence to others was not abated by the consciousness of his own superiority
>
> His ambition was pure from all selfish motives; the love of power and the passion of fame were in him subordinate to his view of public utility

■ Be the change you want to see

At the centre of any desire for significant change is the fundamental task: you have to change yourself. Look at your epitaph and identify which aspect of it is most aspirational to you. Which aspect of it is the biggest jump from where you are now?

Your task is to *Be the change you want to see*. Don't wait until everything is in order. What one thing would you most like to change about yourself based on the work we have done so far? Spend a day, tomorrow perhaps, just noticing that, not yet trying to change but just noticing the gap.

By the end of the week make a new pattern, start a new habit, live a day of your life being the change you want to see and noticing the reaction of others and how you feel. Develop a clear and detailed picture of the change you want to see in yourself. Think about how that will manifest itself in the way you think, the pitch and tone of your voice, your posture, the clothes you wear, the company you seek, what you tell yourself, what you tell others, and how you are with others.

The successful person knows when to ease up

Chapter 7
Cultivating health and well-being

❏ Achieve positive results

❏ Great news on exercise

❏ Take ownership of your plan

❏ Restore your balance

To feel fit and healthy it's necessary to find a balance between conflicting desires and needs, wants and capabilities. Quite often the changes you need to make are small but have to be applied consistently to achieve positive results in your total well-being. By making small changes you can reap huge benefits.

The first element necessary is to understand what you want to do and achieve, which is why this book first of all asks you to look at your vision, your sense of purpose, your needs, your values.

If you aspire to be a great sportsperson then what you eat and when, and what fitness regime you follow, are likely to dominate your life. Those who have made it to the top of their profession, especially in sport, have an imbalance of life – or so it might seem to someone who works 9 to 5, watches TV three nights a week, does sport twice a week and sees friends three nights a week.

Some people can defer balance for a while to achieve their goals but it is important to keep yourself fit and healthy whatever your focus. There are foods that will enhance health, well-being and fitness, and others, when taken in excess, that will upset that balance. Good diet and regular exercise facilitate maintenance of a healthy body weight, enhance well-being and reduce the risk of heart disease, stroke, some cancers, diabetes and osteoporosis.

The decision of what to eat for authentic health needs to be made on the basis of nutrition and vitality. Earlier we worked through some exercises to gain clarity and get in touch with what you want to be. Now you need to ask how you are going to feed yourself and look after yourself to help you get there. Good food needs to be safe, nutritious, varied and enjoyable. It should enhance and improve our lives and give us the capability to achieve all we want.

A basic healthy diet

The building blocks of nutrition are carbohydrates, proteins and fat. Vitamins and minerals are essential components of a diet that not only prevents deficiency but optimises health and may actually reduce the risk of certain diseases.

All meals should be based on foods rich in complex carbohydrates for sustained energy and to minimise swings in blood-sugar levels. Complex carbohydrates are also a good source of fibre, B vitamins (which help you utilise energy from foods), some iron and calcium. Some fat in the diet is essential but most people need to eat less. Choose fats and oils containing monounsaturates (such as olive and rapeseed oils), and try to reduce intake of animal fats (in meat and dairy products such as hard cheeses) which are high in saturates. In addition, try to incorporate oily fish into your diet as the type of fats found here, known as omega-3 fatty acids, are known to be beneficial for your heart. Changing the fat content of your diet, while limiting overall intake, particularly if you are over-weight, will be a positive step towards maintaining a healthy cholesterol level and cardiovascular system.

▓ Fruit and vegetables

The current advice is to eat at least five portions of fruit and vegetables each day. What happens if you eat a sandwich for lunch one day and a pizza or curry for dinner – do you eat 10 portions the next day? You should be aiming for a balance and choosing foods that incorporate salads, vegetables or fruits. Fresh, frozen, dried and canned all count, as do all fruit and vegetable juices.

To start the day with maximum nutrition use/get a juicer – vitamins and minerals are absolutely best provided in fresh fruit and vegetables. This is because there are many unknown compounds in fruit and vegetables which we don't yet know much about. What we do know is that all evidence points towards a regularly good intake of fruit and vegetables being protective against developing some cancers and heart disease, the western world's number 1 killers. They are also incredibly low in calories and high in fibre so can help to satisfy hunger and keep your gut healthy, without contributing significantly to calorie intake. However, if you do not meet your target intake often, or are par-ticularly stressed, then a general multivitamin and mineral supplement taken daily is a suitable replacement.

▓ Fluid

An adult should consume approximately two litres per day, although this varies according to age, climate, diet and physical activity. This includes water and other drinks like squash and tea. Some fluid comes from the foods we eat and these count too. Fluid is vital to keep all the cells in your body well hydrated and functioning in optimally. Feeling tired, having persistent headaches and even feelings of hunger between meals can all be caused by a lack of fluid.

■ Caffeine and alcohol

Caffeine, found in coffee, tea, chocolate and cola, is a stimulant. It has been found in studies to have beneficial effects on performance, sustaining attention and alertness. Abstinence in regular consumers can have negative effects such as muddy-headedness due to the negative effects of 'withdrawal' symptoms.

It is important to be moderate with intake – while the odd cup of tea or coffee will cause no detrimental effects, to prevent a dehydrating effect, drink a glass of water with strong coffee. If you find you are too dependent on your daily 'caffeine kick', then try to look at the reasons for this: for example, stress, tiredness, inability to concentrate; and get to the root of the problem. If you want to try to cut down, it is best to wean yourself off gently to prevent withdrawal headaches.

■ Exercise

There is great news on exercise! Research now says that a simple 20 minutes of gentle exercise a day is all that's needed to maintain mental health. Your well-being and stress management will be greatly enhanced by 20 minutes walking outside each day. For the body, a little more is required, but you do not have to beat yourself up over this. Find what exercise you like and stick to it – there are so many different forms of exercise, including walking, cycling, yoga, tai chi, dance, badminton, martial arts, tennis, skating, football, running, rugby and netball.

Just take a ten-minute stroll in a park or the countryside as a quick way of healing yourself. New research on exercise says 'mindful' or 'mindless' exercise should be chosen according to the precise nature of your stressed condition. If you feel anxious or depressed take up exercise that is 'mindful', where you have to concentrate upon the movement or your breath, such as in swimming. Other 'mindful' exercises include yoga, ballet, tai chi and pilates. If you are momentarily stressed, 'mindless' exercise is best, such as running, playing football or going to the gym.

Exercise may improve mental health by helping the brain cope better with stress. Evidence suggests that physically active people have lower rates of anxiety and depression than sedentary people. Contrary to popular belief, there is little evidence that exercise causes a rush of endorphins, but norepinephrine is released, and this chemical is thought to have a major role in modulating the neurotransmitters that play a part in stress response. It seems exercise thwarts depression and anxiety by enhancing the body's ability to respond to stress.

Remember, though, that stress is the umbrella term for a lot of disorders. You first have to find what is causing the problem, then determine the precise stress reaction, then work out the most appropriate stress avoidance or management technique. While exercise is helpful, it can't replace what psychotherapy offers – the gradual shift in cognition and emotion that helps one cope better – but it can work alongside therapy very well indeed.

The good news with exercise and stress management is that you don't have to exercise until you sweat and overexert yourself to reap mental benefits. Psychologists are discovering that how much or how intensely one exercises is not the key factor in relieving depression and anxiety. In addition, exercise can give non-threatening social support. It is quite levelling to be alongside someone else in just shorts, T-shirt and trainers – your ego isn't bound up with status dressing or what you do for a living. It has an equalising effect that is good for generating feelings of social acceptance.

Exercise should be managed carefully to ensure that recovery is complete after each session and that capability is not stretched so far as to cause injury. Aerobic exercise is good for the heart but needs to be eased into if you are unused to it. Aerobic exercise basically is where you are working your heart 70–80 per cent of its maximum, minus your age. Such exercise is usually fast cycling or cycling up hills, running, swimming at your maximum and rowing. With aerobic exercise you need to measure your heart rate – the best advice is to go to your local gym and get yourself tested so that you become aware of when you are in an aerobic state and when you are not. You don't want to tax your heart, you want to tone it.

Anaerobic exercise involves short, intense bursts of activity, such as weightlifting, which pushes the body to use a different metabolic pathway than the oxygen-bound system of aerobic activity. It is essential to get good aerobic capacity before moving onto weight-bearing exercises so I would recommend a one-month programme of aerobic exercises with each session lasting between 20 and 45 minutes and starting and finishing with a good stretching session. Aerobic sessions should be varied and include a rest day in between to ensure the trained muscles are fully recovered.

Weight training should be supervised at a local gym where a programme designed to meet your particular exercise needs will increase personal gains and minimise the chance of injury. Good exercise will improve the benefits of a healthy diet and increase capacity, energy and feelings of well-being. If well timed around meals it will also improve the absorption of nutrients, elimination of waste products and repair of muscle.

As a way of getting rid of stress energy, nothing beats aerobic exercise. When the body meets a possible threat to its equilibrium it kicks into self-protection and provides us with the strength and energy to either fight or run away from danger. We rarely use this inbuilt 'fight or flight' mechanism, and the result is that the body goes into a state of continually cycling high energy. When there is nowhere for that energy to go the body can stay in a state of over-arousal for hours at a time. Exercise is the most logical way to dissipate this excess energy.

If you can exercise immediately after you are aware of acute feelings of stress, so much the better, but regular exercise, every day or at least every other day, will still drain off excess stress. At the very least, it is important to exercise three times per week for a minimum of 30 minutes each time. For chronic or acute stress, exercise is an essential ingredient in any stress-reduction programme – there's absolutely no doubt that you will feel better if you take the right amount and kind of exercise.

■ Party! Hang out! Have fun!

Let go in a good indulgence every week. Do something you really enjoy, and this can mean taking up a new interest or hobby. You will meet all sorts of people, get different perspectives, keep your mind open and achieve an important aspect of work–life balance.

Those who have a good network of reliable and supportive friends can withstand a lot of life's ups and downs with equanimity. If things aren't going well for you, to prevent yourself feeling a bit down – don't hide from your friends. Phone them, see them, spend time with them.

Many otherwise rational people think nothing of working from dawn to dusk without taking breaks, but this isn't sustainable – we need to learn to monitor our stress and energy levels, act on the information and pace ourselves. The successful person knows when to ease up.

■ A five-step programme to restore your balance

You may have been thinking of taking steps to improve your health and fitness for a while and may even have made some attempts. It is time now to really challenge your previous habits and beliefs. Try to stay with this new way of living for four weeks; the effects on your sense of well-being and bodily health will be so clear that you will be able to make a judgement on how important your personal balance is to you.

As you learn to follow the recommendations, your energy levels will increase and become more stable, your fitness routines will become easier, stress symptoms will ease and sleep will become deeper and more restorative. This will help you build a strong foundation and a creative path for all other aspects of your life's ambitions and dreams.

Step 1: Sort out your environment

Take a look at your food cupboard and throw out what is not in the nutritious category – biscuits, junk food, prepared food. Go shopping for complex carbo-hydrates and nuts as snacks. Clear a space for the fresh fruit and vegetables and the juicer on the top of your kitchen counter – in prime position.

Use magnets or sticky notes to fasten encouragement messages or images to your fridge door. It is important to think of the longer-term consequences of your actions: imagining how you will feel an hour from now, ten hours, six months – if you do what you are about to do. An encouragement might be a picture of the clothes you want to get into, or someone running along the beach, or a picture of a lovely holiday resort you intend to go to with the money you saved on stopping snacking (and stopping smoking, come to that).

Tell those around you calmly and seriously what you want, what you intend and ask them to encourage you. Listen to the ones who do. Ignore the rest.

Step 2: Work out a plan for your new behaviour

Work out what you want to achieve, what it will do for you, and why you want/need it. Write down your vision of yourself, how you will look and feel at the end of your programme. Now work backwards from there to where you are now and mark out weekly goals. Then work out milestones – and how you are going to celebrate them. Finally, work out exactly what you are going to do to achieve those goals, and plan it into your schedule – and other people's. If you have dinner at someone's house planned – let the host know about your programme. If you need to make arrangements to clear your diary so that you can do your exercise or meditation in peace, do that. Take ownership of your plan, be accountable for it.

What exercise are you going to do that you haven't yet tried? How are you going to plan in your exercise time? Avoid exercise for two hours after a meal; eat within the hour after exercise; remember to take water to drink while exercising; take some fruit to eat an hour either side of the exercise.

Take most of your nutrition before 8pm at night, if possible. If you are busy all day, take regular snacks of high-protein nuts and seeds, vitamin- and mineral-packed fruit – some five portions – and have a vegetable soup or salad for lunch. Then in the evening you can have a light carbohydrate meal like pasta with sauce or risotto or steak and salad.

Work out what you are going to do when you feel like relapsing. The most common time to relapse on a commitment is early in the project – more than half of New Year resolutions are broken by February. So you need to develop a strategy that will help you overcome your urges to give up. Try something like this affirmation: 'Every time I feel like eating chocolate I will drink a glass of water and either walk around the block or phone a relative/friend.' In doing this you will be setting up a system for your self-control. It is vital to stop a little lapse before it becomes a serious one and you think you've blown it for the day so you might as well really go for it! Instead, stop the relapse as soon as you can and get back on track with your plan.

Step 3: Find and use ways to motivate yourself
Spend five minutes each day thinking about how you will look, walk, talk, act, feel after you have succeeded in following your fitness programme

At the start of a meal, calm yourself with a couple of deep breaths. Feel good about showing the strength to make good choices.

Focus your attention on your accomplishments. Take small steps and make sure you congratulate yourself. Be kind to yourself if you relapse. Talk calmly and encouragingly to yourself. Instead of criticising yourself, say things like: 'It's OK, it's just one step back, you can get back on track again. You can do this.' Some people swear by daily affirmations: 'I eat and drink what is good for me.' 'I do exercise because it makes me fit and healthy.' Create your own: the things you know that work for you.

You will find it easier to make the right choices if you get yourself into the mindset of being that person (who is part of you, after all!) who is fit and healthy. Notice what it does for you, how much easier it is to make the right choices and how much more calm vitality you have as a result.

Step 4: Remember it is not only what you eat but why and how

Understanding why you do what you do is vital in managing your behaviour and mood. Doing the wrong thing for your health is not about greed or laziness in my experience. If you look at it more closely, you might find that you crave whatever it is that gives you a shot of what you need momentarily even though you don't like, and often ignore, the after-effects. Try to think ahead – you know that the instant high won't last.

Ask yourself when thinking about the habit you want to break: 'What needs and emotions are connected with this habit? How else can I satisfy or let go of those needs?' Don't kid yourself that this behaviour is just 'you' and that you were born this way – remember in between the stimulus and response is a space and in that space is your power.

Step 5: For one month make these foods your key focus

First of all: fresh, seasonal, locally produced foods – that means don't buy imported strawberries in winter. Secondly: organic, humanely reared meats and fish from local butchers and fishmongers who can tell you where the food comes from. Thirdly, eat at least five portions of vegetables and some fruit every single day. Catch up if you miss a day. Clean all fruits, salad, herbs and vegetables carefully, especially if they are not organic, to wash off chemicals. Avoid processed foods, caffeine, alcohol and high-fat, sugary and salted foods. Drink 2 litres of water daily. Drink water half an hour before but *not* with a meal, as this is said to dilute the digestive enzymes. Try it and notice the difference.

If you need to take steps to deal with stress, the next chapter will offer you tried and tested strategies that you can use every day.

Manage the cause of stress and your reactions to it

Chapter 8
Stress management and strategies

❏ Get to the root of the stress

❏ Relieve symptoms and deal with the cause

❏ Regain optimism and equilibrium

❏ Learn beneficial management strategies

Overworking and being busy all the time has become a modern preoccupation. In the US, Japan and the UK there is a well-established culture of working long hours. If you are a manual worker, there are positive benefits in term of increased earnings; in management and the professions, these benefits include better promotion prospects and greater job security.

If you are suffering from the pressure of working long hours you will feel the demands of what you have to do. Sometimes it can be quite uplifting and even exciting for a while. In anything but small doses, however, most people find overworking is exhausting, even if you have high energy. Acute stress sometimes feels exciting but cannot be maintained for long.

Deadlines, challenge and even our frustrations and sorrows add depth and enrichment to our lives. To have no stress at all would be a depressant and would leave us feeling bored, dulled or apathetic; on the other hand, excessive stress may leave us feeling vexed and confused. It is possible to manage the cause of stress and your reactions to it – to be motivated, but not overwhelmed, and this is a very individual thing. What is overwhelming distress to one person is excitement to another; what excites you at one stage in your life might have overwhelmed you at an earlier stage.

By getting to the root causes of your stress, you can both relieve current problems and symptoms and also prevent recurrences. To really manage stress, the unpalatable fact is you have to do something different, you have to change. You have to identify what causes you to feel stressed and how stress manifests itself, and then change it.

Emotionally we might feel rejected, angry, depressed, worried, fearful, irritable, impatient; there is a tendency to act impulsively and not in the best interests of ourselves or others.

Physically we feel tired, often with headaches, irritable bowel, skin disorders, aches and pains in the shoulders, neck, legs and back, insomnia, ulcers, heart palpitations, cold extremities, sweating, high blood pressure, colds, heart disease, and even stroke.

Cognitively we are affected because our concentration is decreased and we suffer memory loss, indecisiveness, confusion – our minds can go blank or race without clarity; there is a loss of sense of humour and the ability to keep things in perspective.

Behaviourally people fidget; nervous habits like fiddling with clothes, nail-biting or tapping fingers is increased; we can be blunt and rude to people; unhealthy choices may be made regarding diet, smoking and drinking, and there might be an increase in rash, self-destructive behaviour.

The strategies that you can consider adopting to manage stress depend on the source of that stress. If you feel stressed, you need to get to the root cause, and then it will be possible to do one of two things: you can change the problem or change how you feel about it.

The 'Serenity Prayer' reflects this very well:

> *God, grant me the serenity to accept the things I cannot change,*
> *Courage to change the things I can,*
> *And the wisdom to know the difference,*
> *Living one day at a time,*
> *Enjoying one moment at a time,*
> *Accepting hardships as the pathway to peace.*

■ Changing the problem

If you are feeling low, negative or out of sorts and it's possible to actually do something to change the situation, that's helpful. If you are unable to make a decision, try talking to someone who will be able/qualified to help you see things more clearly – a coach, a friend, a family member, a counsellor or a therapist. Procrastination itself can cause a lot of stress and if this is your situation you may have to take back some control – this will be easier if you have some support until you feel that you are on track again.

Some problems unravel in time but can be wearing in the meantime – if you are caught up in a long-term painful situation, such as a relationship break-down or divorce settlement, it will help if you distract yourself and try to maintain equilibrium by pursuing hobbies, spending time with friends, engaging in productive and meaningful work, and doing exercise to relieve the stress.

Changing the problem may involve moving away from it, changing your lifestyle choices or changing your behaviour to impact on it.

Can you change the cause of the stress by avoiding the person or situation?
Can you reduce the intensity of it or shorten your time in this situation?
Who can you ask to help you or share this with safely?
What have you tried so far – what can you do differently?
Do you need help in changing your behaviour?

All of this requires emotional intelligence – knowing yourself and managing your emotions. It takes moral courage, assertiveness, time and money management, a reliable support network, good problem-solving techniques and decision-making tools.

■ Changing how you feel about the problem

Changing how you feel about something often involves changing your thinking about it. Your interpretation and response to something that causes you stress is not rooted and dependent solely on an external event; it greatly depends upon how you perceive the event and the meaning you give to it. So, how you look at a situation determines if you will respond to it as threatening or challenging.

Try to be absolutely clear about what precisely is causing you stress and how it manifests itself in your symptoms.

Write down the things or situations that have caused you stress recently. Keep a diary and note when you felt stressed, describing as clearly as you can the precise cause of the stress and your reaction.

Make a point of noticing when you are stressed – the situations, the people, the environment. It is important to pay attention to it and to the stories you tell yourself about it instead of ignoring it or shrugging it off. Analyse the stress in order to manage it successfully.

Make a note of what happens to you mentally, physically and emotionally when you are affected by these various forms of stress. How do you feel and what do you do when you feel this way – do you make a cup of coffee, go out for chocolate (or raid your stores ...), call up a friend, open a bottle of wine?

Question your mental reasoning: decide whether you are being realistic or perhaps making assumptions, overdramatising, overgeneralising or have got stuck in a rigid way of seeing things.

Ask yourself if you have unreasonable expectations of others and/or of yourself. Are you trying to please everyone?

Ask yourself how else you could see this situation and what could be the positive outcomes.

You *can* work it out. You are good at coping. You have adapted in the past well. Remember all the things you have coped with in your life. Either list them now or go back to a list you made before.

■ Analysing your time management

If you have a problem getting everything done, ask yourself what is really causing this difficulty? Is it a question of time management. Discover the root cause and overcome it. Answer each of these questions, think through the origins and how to reach a workable solution that you feel happy with.

Delegation

Is it that I don't trust people easily?

How can I learn to?

How is my management and follow-up of delegated work?

What disciplines do I need to adopt?

Is it that I do not have enough information about my team's capabilities?

How can I securely find out about them and their abilities?

Decision-making

Do I like to put off making a final commitment?

How have I approached making commitments in the past?

Am I uncomfortable making decisions without all the information I think I need?

How can I learn to stop gathering information and make the decision?

Am I afraid of making a wrong decision?

What is the fear here, where is its base and is it irrational?

What do I need to get over?

Planning

Am I taking the time up front to plan in all the things I need to do/achieve?

Am I assessing and updating my yearly, monthly, daily schedules?

Do I work on important things at the best time of the day for me?

Stress

Do I feel healthy, with enough sleep and good nutrition?

Have I had enough exercise lately?

Am I doing too much or putting too much emphasis on one part of my life?

Assertiveness

Do I get called to meetings I don't need to go to?

Do I get interrupted by telephone calls too much?

Do I spend a lot of time reading?

Role clarity

Do I know what is expected of me and what is exceptional performance?

Do I have clear goals?

■ Five tools for managing stress

There are some very simple and almost universal ways you can reduce, manage and prevent stress. Here is a list of some practical and down-to-earth strategies. Most of them can be applied easily, while others are a little more involved. All have been found to be beneficial.

1 **Build up your health and fitness**

2 **Build a supportive network**

3 **Reassert your priorities on your schedule**

4 **Take time out for yourself**

5 **Check and manage your thoughts – use the AMULET in Chapter 5.**

Step 1: Build up your health and fitness

Try to take the advice in the health and fitness section. If your body is malnour-ished or unfit you will not be able to manage stress well. Put in some effort and discipline here and it will serve as a wonderfully firm foundation for your well-being and the ability to live the life you want.

Make sure you are getting enough sleep. If you have enough sleep you will wake feeling refreshed, have enough energy during the day to do what you need, sleep undisturbed and wake naturally before the alarm goes off in the morning. Too much sleep, on the other hand, can make you feel lethargic. You need to test to find out for yourself what works for you.

Step 2: Build a supportive network

We all need a friend we can trust. If your current friends do not fit that descrip-tion, try to meet some new people. It is sometimes helpful to have friends who share your current sense of purpose and values and meet the sense of where you are now – and these friends might be new. Old friends are great for remind-ing us who we are outside of our jobs and roles – they love us for who we are, not what we do.

If you are having trouble at work, old friends can be wonderfully grounding and reassuring for your future. Make time to see an old friend.

If you have moved into a new job or neighbourhood, remind yourself that anyone in a new environment goes through an adjustment phase. Resist the urge to withdraw from people, especially if you are a single person living alone. Instead, practise your social skills by making a daily effort to engage with some-one. Be positive, enthusiastic, thoughtful and encouraging. Look for connections between you. Maximise your chances of opportunity by getting out and about, and be open to new experiences.

Step 3: Reassert your priorities on your schedule

Work out what you really want and need. This means looking at your sense of purpose and how that breaks down into the way you are spending your time. There are some very basic time management tips that work for most people.

Write down your yearly goal, then break that down into monthly goals and milestones. Work out how that is going to be achieved on a weekly and daily basis. Each day write down what you have to do and what you want to achieve, and remind yourself how you want to be – what style you want to have, what attitude you want to give out.

Be clear about your intention and what you want to portray. Then work out which job it is important to make sure you achieve, and which job is urgent. It is very helpful to work out alongside each item how long you think it will take you – then you can calculate that, for instance, all the tasks you intend to do today will take you 40 hours and you can clearly identify you are being over optimistic.

Take seven sheets of paper. Put 'am' and 'pm' at the top on the left and right of each sheet, and write down what you did and how much time it took. If you want to do a deep analysis, use a grid and log every fifteen minutes. If you find it helpful, colour-code the things you have done in categories to create a clear way of seeing where your time goes. It can be very enlightening to do this. All of this requires work on your part – but the first step to making wise choices is clear information, not assumptions. If you put in the effort now, it will benefit you later.

If you have a meaningful goal, don't give up on it. Keep on practising, pushing, prioritising. As Pythagoras said:

Choose always the way that seems the best, however rough it may be. Custom will soon render it easy and agreeable.

You can also use imagery to rehearse before a big event, allowing you to run through the event in your mind. You can even incorporate the odd event that might happen so that you are prepared to handle the unexpected. This is a technique used very commonly by top sports people, for example, who learn good performance habits not only by doing them physically but also by mentally visualising repeated performances. Visualisation can put you in touch with the future, what it will feel like when you have achieved your goals, giving you the motivation and self-confidence to continue.

If your goal conflicts with what others need of you, you need to be brave enough to have the conversation with them. Tell them about your needs and desires and listen to theirs. Work together on how you can constructively build a way forward. If you don't talk about it, misunderstandings, resentments and guilt arise, and all of those things produce stress.

Step 4: Take time out for yourself

Take time out to listen to your hunches by meditating, clearing your mind or taking a walk. The next time you have a decision to make, go for a long walk and, as soon as you come back, record your thoughts: write them down. This helps to clarify them, and also helps you to remember them.

Relaxation methods work on the basis that you cannot be relaxed and stressed out at the same time. So force yourself into a state of relaxation if necessary. The deep-breathing technique – deliberately taking deep, slow, controlled breaths – usually works.

Muscular relaxation also works in the same way. Deliberately and consciously tense all your body and then let it go and relax. Or start at the bottom and work up: tense your feet and ankles and then let them go. Then tense the calves and knees and relax them. Work right up the body through the thighs, the buttocks, the stomach, up the vertebrae, shoulders, neck, face, tongue, tensing for a few seconds, then relaxing.

Do something simple and pleasant that requires little thought. For example, strolling in the sun, or wrapping up well and taking a short walk whatever the weather, sitting by a lit fire, gently stroking a cat, lying on a hammock. Any absorbing hobby – gardening, cooking, painting, sewing – can do the trick.

Take a daytime nap. The classic power nap is only 5–20 minutes. More time may give you the rest you need but it could disturb your evening sleep, and it is likely that if you nap for longer than half an hour you will wake up feeling groggy and disorientated. Taking time out to distract yourself from what's bothering you will not magically resolve the problem, but it will give you a chance to lessen the physical effects of stress, and that will help you deal more effectively with whatever's causing the problem.

Short time-out breaks, such as walking around your workplace, listening to a song if you can, having a chat to someone, stepping outside for some fresh air and a change of scene – gentle, leisurely, uncomplicated ways to have some respite from focused attention or pressure – can greatly improve your concentration and enhance your productivity.

Step 5: Check your thoughts and manage them

A strong mediator of how we are affected by stress is our ability to be effective and impact on something – this is called your *locus of control*. Think back to all the times you have made an impact in a situation. Generate as many as you can, no matter how small. Consider writing them down.

Look for the positive in every situation. Turn your bad luck into good by reframing it or seeing the positive side. if you look for what you can learn from it, you will have reframed the situation and reclaimed your power. By changing the way you see something, you change the way you feel.

Remember, you have the power to choose how you feel.

In order to get in touch with our rational logic and think creatively, we need first to access our self-esteem and self-efficacy. It will be helpful to think back to the times you exhibited strong resolve, made tough decisions and were influential and resourceful.

■ Get in touch with your humour

Humour can be a potent and creative stress reducer. Reframing is a useful technique to access our humour, and laughter is known to relieve tension. Carefully controlled studies show that laughter lowers cortisol levels, increases the amount of activated T lymphocytes and increases the number of T cells that have helper/suppresser receptors. In short, laughter stimulates the immune system, offsetting the immuno-suppressive effects of stress.

The emotions and moods we experience directly affect our immune system, so gaining emotional intelligence and control over our moods is essential for our health. Having a good sense of humour allows us to perceive and appreciate the incongruities of life and provides moments of joy and delight.

■ Expect good fortune

Show some trust and faith. You get more of what you focus on, so think about what you have been focused on lately that has been helpful and what hasn't.

What could go well in your life soon?
Who do you need to open up to or who can you ask for help?

Now visualise that going very well in as much detail as possible.
Trust yourself.

Resist the temptation to race on. Take a break here and now and write in detail about that good thing you expect to happen:

■ Appraisals and moving on

Do an appraisal of those around you for their integrity, their capability and motivation. If they come up trumps, trust them. If not, work with them for a while, give them a chance and then if things don't improve, find a way to separate yourself, break the pattern and move into a new energetic phase.

Another way of checking your thoughts is to question your fairness. Are your goals and expectations realistic? Are you expecting too much of yourself? What are you trying to prove, what do you need?

Are you perhaps overreacting to someone's errors? Have you let them know what you expected? Have you heard their intentions? Do they even know they've upset you or disappointed you?

Are you worrying a bit too much here, seeing the negative side of something only? Are you expecting this to go wrong because something in the past, unconnected, went wrong?

What are you assuming is true? What do you think someone else could be assuming? How could you see this differently to explain it?

If you want something and then shy away from it, what is it that you find attractive and what does that give you? And what is it that you fear? Is that honestly a rational fear, given the evidence of the situation? What more information do you need?

The key to moving on is forgiveness, being compassionate, letting go. As someone said, 'The future hasn't happened, and the past is not going to happen again', so being here in the now is a wise strategy and attitude. Plan and prioritise as best you can, and then be easy on yourself.

■ Dealing with long-term stress

Chronic stress is unrelenting demands and pressures that go on for seemingly interminable periods of time. People often endure chronic stress if they have experienced childhood trauma, loss or a traumatic end to an important relationship early in life. Such experiences can be profoundly affecting, and can lead a person to set up walls of defences and rigid rules for living that are intended to protect that person's feelings from there on.

By learning, instead, how to regain and maintain an optimistic attitude, you can avoid depression and actually improve your mental and physical health.

Learning to find optimism again, taking care of yourself and breaking out of negative and limiting thought patterns can bring about deep healing and real transformation.

From surveys by the World Health Organisation and the Institute of Work, we know that up to 50 per cent of the workforce are unhappy in their job at any one time. A review by psychiatrists showed that 75 per cent of breakdowns can be traced to stress at work. Nearly one in three marriages in the UK ends in divorce, one of the most stressful life events. A recent UK work–life balance survey estimated that three in ten employees experience a mental health problem in any one year, mainly as a result of anxiety. While the new family-friendly legislation in the UK is welcome, the issue of work–life balance is fundamental for all individuals – a healthy balance is vital for everyone, not only for those with young children.

If you are under constant stress at work, it's usual to take it home, and that could have a detrimental effect on personal relationships, which in turn affects how you feel on returning to work. If this is happening to you, you can break the cycle. If you've had a bad day at work, try to relax briefly before you go home (even if you live alone and only have the cat or the goldfish to take it out on). Breathe deeply out and in, and go for a brisk walk if possible to clear your head. Even simply telling yourself to let it go – or giving yourself permission to let it go – can help release some of the tension.

If you think you are suffering from more than average stress, consider consulting a professional. Many people live with chronic anxiety and depression, but with support and encouragement you can learn to manage and relieve the symptoms. If you ask your doctor for help, the chances are you will be offered medication. A more creative alternative might be to seek professional help from a psychotherapist or chartered clinical psychologist.

■ Use visualisation

Using your creative imagination can be a potent method of stress reduction. Our blood pressure varies dramatically with what we are thinking, so you can use imagery to reduce your blood pressure and feel calmer throughout your whole body, especially if you combine exercise, visualisation and meditation. Do the deep breathing and muscular relaxation (see page 125) first, then imagine a very peaceful scene – for example, looking at a lake, or being on a beach, in a lovely garden, on top of a mountain range. It can be a real place or you can make it up. Imagine the picture life-size, make the colours bold and bright, listen to the sounds – do you hear peace, birds, waves, ripples? What do you smell – salt water, earth, flowers?

◼ Meditation

Meditation is a personal quiet time, a process and state of relaxation, reflection and contemplation. During meditation the stress reactions are reversed: pulse slows, blood pressure falls, breathing slows and muscles relax. It has calming effects, often generating greater presence, confidence, a feeling of tolerance, connection and self-control.

Meditation makes no demands on the mind. Sometimes, when it is unburdened of pressing everyday demands, decisions or problems to solve, the mind clears away confusion and becomes creative. When the mind is left to itself the unconscious often raises important topics and gives us deeper understanding, insight or a perspective. Meditation takes practice and, to really benefit, some commitment. There are many good books, centres and groups where you can find out more about meditation. The following is a basic everyday practice.

Set aside half an hour each day. Select a time when you can be quiet, undisturbed – this could be a room in your house or a place of worship or a private spot outdoors. Sit in a relaxed position – in the traditional cross-legged position if that is comfortable, otherwise sit in a straight-backed chair. The spine should be straight and feet should be on the floor. The eyes can be closed or slightly open, and if you wish you can light a candle to help you focus and clear your mind. Sit quietly for a minute or so, breathe easily, letting your body relax and your mind forget all external and internal pressures.

If you find yourself thinking, just say very gently and calmly to yourself, 'thinking!' and bring your attention back to the breath. In this way, the mind and body are connected through the breath.

At first you may find you can only sit for a short time, but within, say, a month of daily practice this will increase. If images, memories, fantasies or plans come into your mind, allow them to pass without attaching to them; respond gently and just go back to focusing on the candle or breathing or sound. If an important thought comes in, you will remember it later. Stay relaxed in an attitude of mind that is quiet, calm, respectful, alert, open, interested, optimistic, and tolerant of whatever arises as you sit.

When you are ready, come out of your meditation slowly. Open your eyes, gently stand and stretch up. Slowly allow yourself to start to think again but try to let this gentle state of mind continue for a few minutes and notice how you feel simultaneously relaxed and alert, calm and energised.

Prioritise your goals

Chapter 9
Moving towards your goals

❑ Review your vision and mission

❑ Do a reality check

❑ Ensure that your values are lived

❑ Negotiating what you want

By now you will probably know what your work–life balance needs are and be committed to achieving the end results. This chapter will help you in clarifying what you want your outcome to look like. Before you start the ten-step goal-setting process, reflect on the most exceptional thing you've done in the past week, month and year. Where did you make a difference in a way you can be proud of? Start the process with a positive sense of achievement – this will give you a good jumping-off point at which to begin to work towards your goal.

■ Ten-step goal-setting process

These guidelines will be helpful in making a contract with yourself and maintaining the commitment to ensure that you get real benefit from the work you have put in so far, and that you have the level and kind of support and challenge you need. It is essentially about turning your reflections and observations into goals.

Just like the founder of Sony did, you have made statements of purpose, and the time to make them happen is now. You have gone through a process of establishing your vision and mission statements, developing real awareness and understanding on the way. Now we move on to the next phase: commitment and action.

Step 1: What do you really want? What do you really need?

Choose things that you find energising, exciting and compelling. Before you start, look back over the vision and mission exercises and then write down whatever comes into your mind.

....

....

Step 2: Prioritise your most important three goals

Isolate your three most important goals and write them down here:

....

....

....

Step 3: What will you get out of it?

Imagine having achieved one of your goals and ask yourself: 'What will having this goal give me, do for me, get me?' Then do the same for the other two.

Goal 1

What will it do for me?

....

What will it give me?

....

What will it get me?

....

Goal 2

What will it do for me?

....

What will it give me?

....

What will it get me?

....

Goal 3

What will it do for me?

....

What will it give me?

....

What will it get me?

....

....

Step 4: Reality check

Look back over your assets and strengths to ensure that you are capitalising on what you are good at and what you enjoy doing. Can you say:

This fits what I know I can do

This fits with what I know I enjoy doing.

To do this I would need to be good at:

....

Have I really got that skill? To fulfil these requirements, things have to be different, and this is what I am going to do:

....

....

Step 5: Validation

How will you know when you have achieved each of your goals? Be specific and have a validation process that includes tangible sensory-based information. What will you see as you achieve each of your goals, what will you hear, what will you feel? How will you celebrate? Write some ideas down here.

....

....

....

....

Step 6: Whose benefit?

Check to see that having your goals is genuinely for your benefit and doesn't harm others, that you are in control and not dependent on others to achieve it. Also check to see that there aren't any hidden rewards for you in *not* achieving a goal. Think through the benefits of *not* achieving each of your three goals.

Do these goals really fit your vision, your mission (not somebody else's)?

How can you ensure that you are living according to your values?

Step 7: Time frame

Work out how long your goals will realistically take to achieve – a month, six months, a year, three years? Then, working back, identify the major steps you will need to put in place along the way – and write them down here.

....

....

....

....

....

Step 8: Obstacles

What is likely to get in the way of you achieving your goal?

....

What are you going to need to do to overcome these obstacles?

....

Who will you have to become? What kind of character traits will you have to develop?

....

Step 9: Resources and constraints

Now list under all these headings the resources and constraints you have, using as much paper as you need to make a thorough inventory:

knowledge
skills
education
funds
time
support network
health

Step 10: Visualise the result

Take some time now to imagine what all this will look like. What are the associated sounds, senses? Really imagine it – what you will look like, wear, sound like, how you will stand, sit. How will people around you respond to you? Now step into that picture and see from those eyes, hear from those ears and feel how good it feels. From that place, imagine yourself twice as successful again, twice the person you want to be – imagine in full colour a lifesize you, again notice all the details of how you sound, look, how people around you react differently to you and what that feels like. Then step into that picture. Act from there, act as if you are already that person; make the choices that person would make, behave in the manner of that person; notice the reactions of others and notice how you get more of what you want.

■ Consider others too

You may need to make a stand now on what you need to achieve the work–life balance you want – but it will also be necessary to do it in a way that is respectful and sensitive towards others. Most people want to stay open to learning and adapting and so the challenge for us individually and together is to stay flexible in our thinking, remain open to new ideas and to use our creative resources. People might underestimate the importance of the change if you:

a) have been moving away from the situation for a long time (for example, if you have been complaining for years about how stressful your work is but not doing anything to improve your situation);

b) were never really there (for example, if you started a business with your partner but really wanted to spend a year travelling);

c) are only just facing up to telling others what you've known for a long time.

If others are stunned by your decision, while for you it seems radical but within the realms of possibility, the chances are that:

a) you began moving away from your old life a long time ago;

b) you have been planning to make a change in your work–life balance for a long time – but others hadn't realised it;

c) you are now ready to involve others in your plans.

You might find it helpful to practise seeing the situation afresh from different angles. When you learn to challenge and test your frames of references, both at work and at home, you will see dramatically positive consequences: you will overthrow the old ways of doing things, gain energy from redefining the rules and make real progress towards the balance you have been working for.

■ Timing

Try to pick your time carefully. Book a time, if necessary, on neutral territory. Make sure that those you need to talk with will not be too tired, stressed or emotional. Make sure you aren't either. Connect emotionally with them – match your emotional state to their ability to receive it. Remember that others may need time to catch up with you, and you may need to re-, re- and renegotiate.

If you are not ready to make the decision, delay it a while. Bear in mind that some decisions have to involve a leap of faith. When you took your first job, you didn't know all about the company, your boss, or who you'd have to work with – you took it on a leap of faith. Think back to your most successful relationship – you didn't know all about their desires, their dreams, their style, but you took that first step on a leap of faith. If you are not ready, don't be pushed, buy time to make sure your decision is as good as you are going to get it with the available information. Accept that it's not possible to ever feel completely ready, otherwise you might miss the successive stages that are part of every thorough process of negotiation.

■ Making your case 1: walk-away position

Work out what you need and want in clear, specific and time-framed terms. Then work out your *minimum walk-away position* – the point from which you will not negotiate further. Be clear and resolute on this. Write it down here.

....

....

....

....

■ Making your case 2: other people's needs

Work out what you think the other people in your life need and want. What do you know of their values, dreams, needs, constraints? How are you going to find out the issues that matter to them? You can ask them, or ask others who know them; test out your ideas on others who know the people who will be affected. Try to understand deeply the other people involved: their dreams, their values, their priorities, so that you know the mutual benefits you see really are likely to be of benefit to them.

Then think through their potential arguments, diverse views and the strength of their convictions and feelings.

■ Making your case 3: revision

Revise your position and argument. Test your own flexibility and ability to compromise. It has to be a two-way street. If you are obdurate and imperative, you may have to face resistance now or a rebellion later. Work out what kinds of compromise would be acceptable to you. Align your position explicitly to other people's needs, perspective and values.

■ Making your case 4: delivery

Work out how you will show that what you propose does have mutual benefits. Craft your delivery, work out exactly how you will say it. Find stories, analogies, metaphors that best illustrate your argument – you can't rely entirely on logic, and it will work best if you make an appeal to the heart as well as the head.

Think of five metaphors that describe your issue with work–life balance. Think of an analogy between your problem and something else. Ask yourself what insights or potential solutions the analogy suggests.

Plan to demonstrate how you have made good judgements in the past, how well you executed a joint decision in the past, how you have worked in the best interests of other people and shown integrity and reliability.

Make explicit your credibility – remind even your partner, and certainly someone who doesn't know you well. Actually imagine the steps, what you will wear, how you will sound, how they might react – visualise yourself being just as you want to be, in line with your values, and feel how good it feels.

■ Assertiveness

Assertiveness means acknowledging the situation and your reactions to it, and stating your needs and expectations in a way that doesn't put others down or anger them. Being assertive is a fine balance because overassertiveness in tone or demeanour can come across as being overbearing, demanding, acerbic or bossy, and is often seen as aggressive. In such cases perceived aggression is often met with aggression, whether covert or overt. So if the other person is reacting covertly with passive-aggressive behaviour – getting back at you indirectly, without telling you why – they may appear to be quietly accepting your plans but in reality are ignoring them and your intentions.

Assertiveness requires you to stay calm. It means feeling OK about yourself, respecting yourself and at the same time staying respectful of others.

If you are negotiating some changes, it is possible that others may feel threatened, belittled, disrespected and even angry. If you don't negotiate what you need, you too could end up frustrated and angry. Unless we express anger in a positively assertive way, it can come out in pathological and dysfunctional ways, or as negativity, jealousy, hostility and sulky, cynical behaviour. People who are constantly putting others down, criticising everything and making cynical comments usually haven't learned how to express their anger constructively.

Finding the optimum amount of assertiveness is very useful to you in achieving support for your work–life balance plans. One of the key rules in assertiveness training is to use 'I' words instead of 'you' words. For instance, instead of saying 'You make me mad when you do that. You should ....', say 'When you do X, I feel Y. I would like you to do Z and then I will feel/do B.' State what the problem is and either offer a solution or ask for their engagement in coming up with a solution that works for both of you.

■ Troubleshooting

If there are frustrations in negotiating your work–life balance plan with a significant person in your life, you may find the following advice helpful.

Dealing with anger If you are negotiating with others in your personal life for change to create better work–life balance and you are met with an angry response, it is helpful to remember that people tend to get angry when they feel insulted or criticised. It's natural to get defensive when you're criticised, but rather than fighting back, think about their intention. Often the other person is acting out of feelings of being neglected, undervalued and unloved.

If someone is behaving badly because they feel undervalued, it takes a lot of courage and maturity on your part to be patient with them and compassionate – but the pay-off to you in gaining ground on controlling your work–life balance is huge.

Using humour Humour is a great way to defuse a difficult situation as long as it isn't your habitual response to laugh off problems. It instantly gives a different perspective, sometimes a crazy one, but it can act as a way of breaking the cycle. Sometimes it is a play on words, a wisecrack.

If someone is really irritating you, stop yourself getting aggressive with them by imagining them instead with a bulbous face, pixie ears, gigantic bottom and wobbly walk.

Take a walk As mentioned in the AMULET and the exercise section, a short walk pays massive dividends.

Just being in the same room where you felt the irritation and fury, just being indoors feeling the challenges and responsibilities can make you feel trapped. Getting out into nature or into any change of scene and having some exercise, too, can be hugely beneficial. It gives you time to think of another way to make suggestions and address your work–life balance changes.

Find another route If something you do or say gets a bad reaction, don't go there. Be creative, find another way.

Finding alternatives together Work with others in your life to find a way that your goal can be achieved. If you find that you have reached an impasse and do not seem to be getting through to someone, why not try this exercise? Both of you write down comments in two columns and then compare them. It can be enlightening when you both see what you have written …

> Column 1: What I'm thinking (but not saying)
> Column 2: What is being said.

Is it also important to ask yourself whether you are showing and giving respect. Sometimes we can be so absorbed in our own lives that we may not fully understand and appreciate others' needs and wants. This series of questions may help you look afresh at yourself and the person you are negotiating with and offer you a way to break through a block.

Am I giving quality time and attention?

Am I getting quality time and attention?

Are my ambitions and needs being treated seriously?

Do I treat theirs seriously?

Do I show attention to what they say?

Do they show attention to what I say?

Do I give absolute attention and listen, really listen?

Are they courteous?

How could I show more courtesy?

Do they jump to conclusions? Have I?

Do they try to put me down? Am I being sarcastic?

Are they pushing their agenda on to me?

Am I being too controlling?

Have they kept their commitments?

Did I keep my promises?

Am I helping them to understand things from my point of view?

How do I show my interest in their well-being?

Is it reciprocated?

Can I imagine what it might be like to be them?

Do I let them know that I understand and care?

How accurate am I when I reflect back their thoughts and feelings?

How many times do they get my intentions and feelings right?

Is their behaviour consistent with what they say? Is mine?

Do they put on a public face? Do I pretend?

Do they open up to me?

Am I being totally, completely honest?

How prepared are they to apologise or admit ignorance? Am I ?

Do they stick to what they have agreed? Do I?

Does their story stack up? Does mine?

■ Be in the right state of mind

In order to have a balanced and fulfilled life it is important to cultivate skill in the management of your state. Your state influences your own behaviour and will determine the results you get with others. Your behavioural flexibility will increase as you learn to manage your own state and that, in turn, will influence others. If you are stiff and uncomfortable, or if you are anxious or hesitant, this will inhibit access to energy, confidence and good decision-making. Positive emotions – such as feeling supported, supporting others, seeing possibilities for a better future – all bring about resourceful states that enable you to maintain creativity, energy, self-esteem and good decision-making abilities.

1 Have the intention to get into a specific state that you think will be helpful; perhaps it is one of being understanding or supportive. To do that, think of a time when you experienced something similar that had a good ending. Take yourself back to that time and imagine the scene lifesize in front of you. Make sure the colours are bright and that the clarity is there; hear the sounds and remember the positive feelings associated with the situation.

Now imagine yourself twice as supportive/understanding (or whatever you think you want to be). See yourself in a lifesize video in front of you being very supportive. How do you stand, sound, breathe, respond? What do you wear? How do you feel? Now step into that. How will you be now in this conversation? You don't have to work it all out beforehand – you can surprise yourself by taking part in a lively dialogue that develops moment by moment. A 'dialogue' has been called a conversation with a centre, not sides: so look for the centre.

2 Explain your intent and what you consider to be common ground – either common goals or common values. Instead of strongly stating your proposition at the outset and trying to push it through, use a little finesse, sensitivity and expect to compromise. Go in prepared, knowing what you want *and* with an open mind. The conversation may go off at tangents but continue to frame your questions and responses around common goals and values.

3 Listen to understand, not to react. Respect the other's view; ask yourself the question, 'How might they see the world that such a view makes sense?' and inquire further. Ask them to share their intention and if this feels different from

the impact they are having, share that – in as unemotional way as possible.

Body language can be useful, but be aware that it does not convey the truth, which is usually complex. Certain things are common – for example, people fiddle with things, flick their feet or touch their nose a lot if they are lying. This is due simply to human physiology: when we lie, there is a rush of blood to the extremities. Changes in posture or expression can be a useful clue, particularly in the heat of an exchange when someone is engrossed in what they are thinking or feeling, and not aware of their body language. For example, if someone who is sitting forward in an open posture suddenly crosses their legs, folds their arms and moves away, it may mean they don't like that part of your proposition.

Having a real dialogue is cathartic, it unburdens the weight of carrying around unspoken thoughts and it releases stress. So try to put things out on the table – this will help both you and the other see things in a different light and encourage the emergence of insights. Create compromise by rethinking and reconfiguring to find the third alternative – the solution that neither of you could have reached alone, and which is the best possible outcome based on active and engaged communication.

You will know
you are motivated
when you wake up
with energy

Chapter 10
Balance, fulfilment and change

❑ Deciding on the right option for you

❑ Look into flexible working

❑ Create your ideal working environment

❑ Going for the balance

Independent working has become a popular alternative in the modern world of work, and it might be the option that offers you the control you need, if you are to achieve a work–life balance that suits you. Going out on your own includes consultancy, becoming self-employed, freelancing, working as an associate or building up a portfolio career.

If you are thinking of going independent, you may be leaving an established and supportive social system as well as an organisation. It may mean that you will no longer have administrative and secretarial support or technical advice. You may be able to share some of those resources, but you may decide to do them yourself, which is often a good thing as it develops flexibility and resourcefulness.

■ Contacts and connections for the independent worker

If you are thinking of going independent, it is important that you stay visible and maintain established connections as well as making new contacts. This will enable you to find energy and pleasure from the social contact you have with colleagues and business associates, as well as keeping you in the front of their minds. Here are a few suggestions that can help to keep your connections alive.

One of the best things you can do if you want more consultancy or freelance work from an organisation is to show your commitment to that business/company. Make yourself visible; offer to do some unpaid work behind the scenes, working alongside the administration team, for example – offer your services wherever there is a need. They will remember you for it.

Write or phone after each piece of work to say thank you. This is always appreciated.

Make a big effort to accept any invitations they give you to parties, celebrations, opening events, client hospitality, community or volunteer events.

Give them something for a change – you give them your work and they pay you in return, but transform the transaction into a partnership: send them an article you have written, a report on a conference you have been to, a review of a book, a profile of a business you know they are going for, or some research you have done on something you know they are interested in.

Ask what they want from you and ask how you could give more – for instance, suggest writing up a progress report, or a debrief on the course you ran or a full report on the meeting you went to or ideas or opportunities they could exploit with or without you.

Independent working has many advantages in the pursuit of a better work–life balance but it can be irregular. It will be helpful if you have a high tolerance for insecurity and uncertainty and are willing to be flexible. It often happens that the lulls are not quiet or relaxing and you might find that at times you become preoccupied either with getting work, or having too much of it.

You will need to be self-motivated, good at initiating meeting new people and able to make an impact quickly, with organisational and communication skills and the ability to be disciplined and stay focused on a task. You will know if you are self-motivated if you wake up with energy. It will also help if you enjoy working alone, sometimes for long periods of time.

A friend recently admitted to me that for all the jibes he used to make about his sales boss getting a cut of his earnings for doing nothing, he has been underachieving without him since he went independent. There was no one there to make him write down his goals, to make him pin them on the notice-board. Without his boss, even though he was a diligent, hard-working independent adviser, he lacked self-motivation; he had no plans and realised that, as a consequence, he had settled for less.

■ Productive downshifting

Downshifting – or changing to a way of working and living that is more pleasurable but less well paid, less demanding and gives you time for rest, recreation and other interests – is becoming an attractive option for many city-dwellers who dream of moving into the country. As long as you know you can cover your living expenses and have enough for contingencies, opting for a lifestyle that is more balanced in its time distribution in a more pleasant and less stressful environment can be an appealing prospect. Sometimes it is a call to the new;

sometimes it is an escape from a current way of living that is no longer entirely satisfying and fulfilling.

Downshifting can be a feasible and enjoyable way of taking care of all the positive needs in your life and minimising their cost and inconvenience. Like any change it needs to be done for the best reasons, whatever this means for you: for example, to spend more time with the family, undergo less stress, engage more in other activities. Deciding what to do is the enjoyable, creative and co-operative part of the process, but before that can be done a realistic financial picture has to be drawn up, prioritised and maintained. Downshifting might involve flexible-working arrangements including fixed-term contracts, part-time work, self-employment, job sharing or a complete change of profession.

Balancing out a new lifestyle is about adopting new values. Look for signs of stress in the family and satisfy small real needs as they appear, even if it means taking part-time work to pay for it. Downshifting succeeds by close attention to detail, finding new and creative ways of doing things and a good degree of discipline. If your downshifting affects others you will need to ask and listen to what they will miss, what they need, and how they will respond, which could be in unexpected ways, to the lifestyle changes.

If you are planning to work at home, the quality of self-discipline will be helpful to you. Some people find working at home a distraction – they find themselves weeding the garden or washing the windows instead of getting down to work. Others find they can't switch off, and while the family are settling down to watch a video, they are quickly sending an email. All of these alternative routes to employment, full or downshifted, require planning and courage, from you and the people around you who might be affected.

■ Negotiating flexible working arrangements

Many firms are seeing the benefit of keeping talented employees and enabling them to work in a way that meets their other responsibilities and/or simply keeps them in good health. In the UK, legislation in 2002 gave parents with children under six and parents of disabled children under 18 the right to ask for flexible working and for that right to be taken seriously. Traditionally it has been women who have wanted to work flexibly but now that men and women are taking on multiple roles, everyone wants more choice about how and when they work.

Flexible working hours might mean that you just want to work in term-time and have all the school holidays off, or it might mean that you agree to 'annualised hours' – working a set number of hours or days per year – or it might mean that you want to job-share. It might mean simply agreeing reduced work time, taking a sabbatical, a break or changing your profession altogether. A possible obstacle is resistance from your employer. You need to be mindful that employers, bosses and peers may not like the idea. They may say things like this:

It is going to mean a lot more management of the schedule
Clients won't be able to get you when they need you
Communication will suffer

They might become envious of your courage, and your time off. They might doubt your commitment to the business/unit and think that you'll just count your hours instead. They might not consider sending you on training courses.

It will help your case if you answer all their queries to their satisfaction and work out a way in which they can be reassured on all fronts. Bear in mind, though, that the employer has a choice whether to agree or not – flexibility can't be imposed by law. A small company might argue that one employee on flexitime has huge implications for productivity – you might find that what is on offer is, for example, a four-day week and a 20 per cent pay cut when you might have wanted to compress the same number of hours into four working days, so be prepared for a possible lengthy process towards a suitable outcome. It will help if you arm yourself with information: for example, in the UK the Institute of Employment Studies found that some small/medium-sized businesses make savings on their budget by implementing flexible work policies because people tend to take less time off sick when they have a better work–life balance.

■ Creative redundancy/unemployment

Sometimes voluntary redundancy is offered to employees when a company is cutting back, and this can be an opportunity as well as a problem. Most often, redundancy involves not just the loss of a job or career but managing the resulting worry and anxiety. If you have been made redundant, you may have gone through a range of emotions from shock and anger to feeling betrayed and doubting yourself. Even if you have been given substantially more than the statutory minimum payment, there is always the worry that you might not be able to pay for your own and your family's basic needs, or find an outlet for your skills and talents and maintain your place in society.

In the UK your job can be made redundant if:

Your employers are ceasing to carry on the business that employs you

They are closing down the site

The business needs fewer people employed to do your job.

Who is to be made redundant should be based upon:

Performance records

Length of service

Disciplinary records and attendance records

Skills and qualifications.

You need to check your eligibility for statutory redundancy – it isn't much. After the initial wave of emotions has gone over you, one of the first practical things you will want to do is examine the financial realities of where you find yourself.

■ First steps in managing finances

Whether you choose to downshift, work part-time, go for voluntary redundancy or you are faced with sudden unemployment, you will probably need to manage your finances differently.

Step 1: List your net assets

Get your paperwork together and create yourself a clear picture of:

all the things you own

any savings

what is in your bank account/s

what equity you may have in your home/s

any investments you have

any dividends you may be due

other sources of income

Step 2: List your outgoings and bills

Have to hand last year's statements and gather all your bills for your living expenses – such things as:

Long-term debts: e.g. mortgage or big loans

Short-term debts: e.g. credit cards and anything hired

School fees

Car loans

Car maintenance: insurance, petrol, tax, MOT, roadside assistance, etc

Insurances: health, income protection, life, medical, home, pensions, etc

Food bills for eating in and out

Holiday: planned and minimum

Maintenance: repairs, replacements and decoration

Clothes for you and the children if you have any

Books, music, cinema, theatre, museums, trips, TV licence

Gifts for birthdays, celebrations

Household services: tax, gas, electricity, water, phones

Hobbies and pastimes

Pets

Doctor and dentist

Licence or professional association fees and insurances

Step 3: Economise

Calculate the total cash cost of servicing all these bills for one year and then look for ways to economise. Take out non-essentials. Look for ways you can reduce certain bills by consolidating debt, buying cheaper or less frequently. This will give you the confidence to conduct your campaign to find a new job or to keep resolute about your new work–life balance choices, and take away one of the main sources of stress in redundancy or downshifting.

Prioritise your expenditure into 'must haves', 'want to haves', 'like to haves' and sheer indulgences, with some movement of how these will change over time.

Change all those little spending habits you've afforded yourself and your family over the years. You can now be more creative about how you get value out of your money, a lesson that will be worthwhile later. If you run separate finances with your partner, be clear of each other's specific responsibilities. Are you utilising the appropriate tax allowances? Are you up to date with your tax bills? Have you saved for any impending tax bill? Are your wills up to date? Have you organised your affairs to mitigate inheritance tax, capital gains tax (this will obviously vary depending which country you live in). Do you have an independent financial adviser?

Step 4: Understand why you have these costs

Get some paper, make two columns and in the left-hand column write down what it is you still need to pay out. In the right-hand column write down why. Ask yourself what it does for you, gives you and whether you really need it.

Make a plan to reduce all spending to the minimum level while satisfying as many people's needs as possible. The two halves of the equation, costs and income, must balance to satisfy the new needs.

Clearing debt of any kind is a useful starting point and a habit that will need to be well controlled in the future. If you have a mortgage, trade-offs will need to be done between cost, space, convenience and what you need to feel secure and at home. Choosing the right time to move and to the right spot affects all future costs and the decision has to be taken carefully. When buying a new house an accurate refurbishment and renewal plan needs to be worked out so that future running costs can be controlled.

The next largest costs are usually the cost of transport and in particular car ownership. Finance and depreciation can be 80 per cent of annual costs; running costs make up the remaining 20 per cent for a car costing £10,000 and replaced every three years. Annual running costs for this same car will be about £1300 per year and most of this expense can be reduced by looking at alternative methods of transport.

Here are some suggestions to get your creativity flowing:

Housing: Reducing the size of housing, moving closer to town centres, moving out to a cheaper area, renting out one or more of your spare rooms.

Transport: Lift shares, walking, cycling, learning maintenance skills, selling your car and renting one when you need one.

Food: Eating out much less, buying supermarket own brands, buying offers, using farmers' markets, buying in bulk, growing your own, picking your own.

Holidays: House exchanges can be found on the web, as can house sitting, YHA, camping, last-minute flights, working holidays, voluntary work.

Pension: Track its value and yields, check it matches your expenses.

Investments: Will they meet long-term needs, are they tax-efficient?

Clothes: Find cheaper outlets, buy unbranded or second-hand, make your own.

Entertainment: Entertain from home, serve home-prepared food, use garden and allotment produce.

Education: Local college night classes, local library, internet, craft classes for cards and small gifts.

Services: Turning thermostats down, getting insulation, grey water recycling, solar water heating, double glazing, triple-A-rated domestic appliances, energy-efficient lights; exchange and borrow tools.

■ Turn redundancy to your advantage

A period of time to yourself will allow you to evaluate your life. It will allow you to get in tune with your family and friends, and encourages creativity if you use it wisely. Put the time to good use by cultivating new and untapped skills. You might find that when you have come through this, you have gained a sense of purpose, a stronger identity and a well-centred and sustainable outlook.

There may not be immediate pressure to find another way of earning money. Initially you even may want to celebrate but eventually you will want to think about your future. Try to stay positive and resourceful – here are a few tips:

eat healthy food
get some exercise every day
read inspirational books
schedule in a holiday
meet up with friends – old and new

New activities and skills can be useful. Decide to give some attention to:

negotiating, communication

trading, borrowing

renting

buying and collecting

de-cluttering

financial planning

trade and craft skills

research and planning

grants and allowances

networking

Use creative redundancy as an opportunity to think again about your career – to understand what else you could do with your interests, passions, energy and transferable skills. Learn new financial, organisational, research, self-improvement, communication, presentation and marketing skills. Take a completely different perspective on yourself, your values and the life you have created; in this situation you can take control and make the best possible adjustments. It's a form of empowerment and responsibility that should not be underestimated, and can be an important stage in finding a work–life balance that suits you in the longer-term.

■ Create your ideal working environment

Your new life will be different and challenging, and you may need to develop new skills. Make sure the changes you make are well thought through and reasonable steps for you to take. In the end the result should be a simpler, happier and stress-free life. You will need not only to manage this stage well but to show how you cope with pressure, chaos, uncertainty.

Use the de-stressing techniques to stay calm, resilient and make the choices that give you positive energy. Be honest with your family and partner about what's happening. You don't have to share all your anxieties with them but you certainly need to give them the opportunity to help you and support you.

If you are working at home, map out your day and make your workspace as comfortable as possible. It is good to treat this as any other job, which may mean starting at 9 and finishing at 5. If that is your preferred pattern of working then keep to it, but you have flexibility now and might want to use it. Surround yourself with all the things you need to do your job well and efficiently.

Make sure that your place of work is as inspirational and pleasant as possible: find a good aspect, get comfortable furniture and storage, happy photos and pictures; play relaxing music if this helps you concentrate. Take time during the day to get some fresh air, exercise and social contact, especially if you are a single person living alone. Avoid the temptation to stay glued to the task every hour of the day – do something that revitalises you and gets you into contact with other people.

◼ Find a mentor
Working independently means that you are responsible for your own career development, and this can be made easier by enlisting the support of a mentor. A mentor is an experienced person willing to share knowledge in a mutually trusting relationship. Their role is one of coaching, counselling, facilitating and networking. A mentor should be someone you respect and value for their experience, style and knowledge, someone you can talk to easily. He/she will act as a sounding board, give advice, be honest and frank, and be prepared to give you constructive feedback

◼ Keep informed and connected
Going to professional association events and conferences not only keeps you up to date but also allows your name to be known in the business.

Invest in being recognised and respected as an active member of a professional organization: this will indicate that you are interested in continuous professional development. When you need help, it will be easier to access.

Pick up information at meetings, workshops, committees. Identify any newspapers and journals that you need to read regularly.

Make presentations, write reports, publish articles, carry out research. Make sure you are in a position to know your market rate, your market worth, the current issues of the day, alternative approaches; expand your network.

■ Do voluntary work

Many associations provide opportunities to give something back to the community. Sometimes such work is rewarded with an invite to tender for paid work, and can lead to other opportunities; usually the reward is a sense of having contributed something worthwhile. These 'feel good' activities are vital in times when you need to remind yourself of how and where you can contribute.

Find out how you can get involved in volunteer work. Sometimes you can take on a new task for a business even on a voluntary basis. It's also possible to initiate something, such as a product or service. Look in local newspapers and join local organisations to find out what might be possible in your area, as well as checking out volunteering options nationally and worldwide with charities and non-governmental organisations like VSO and UNICEF.

■ Consider retraining

If this is one of your options, investigate what the possibilities are in your area. Short courses generally range from one day to a week and may cater to anything from a handful of people to a lecture-theatre full. They tend to be goal directed with the objective of modifying a specific aspect of practice (for example, presentation skills).

There are innumerable external providers of training and the quality can vary dramatically. Seek the advice of the human resource departments you visit, ask your colleagues for their recommendations and/or consult your professional association. Remember to:

ask to talk to previous course participants;

check out the number of people who take part;

find out what the training objectives are and who the trainers are;

find out how feedback is given.

You may also be considering higher degrees or a professional qualification. In this case, find out about the duration of the course, how flexible it is, research its reputation and ask to speak to current and past participants. If you are a woman returner make sure you talk up your skills. Many women need help in realising how easily the skills of home and family management – interpersonal skills, communication, planning, negotiating – can be transferred to a workplace.

■ The skills of networking

The most powerful introductory tool is a personal reference. Networking can be critical at all stages of career development and can be useful in negotiating a better work–life balance. A network is your personal access to specific contacts – not just your business context, past and present. The wider it is the better. It is a source of information and advice, a way to learn about other roles, functions, and cultures, and a way that you might be able to be useful to someone else.

The principles of good networking are to develop a strategy for managing your network; to remember to say thank you and to keep introducers informed; to prepare for all meetings, to seek feedback; to respect confidentiality; ensure that encounters are open and honest; to maintain regular contact; to keep records; to attend conferences, exhibitions, social events and the like to encourage a diverse network.

In preparing for a meeting, you might find the following tips helpful:

Consider the purpose of the meeting (e.g. to negotiate flexible working)
What are your priorities?
How are you going to start? How are you going to generate rapport?
What do you need to prepare or find out?
What do you want to achieve? What are you prepared to accept?
Avoid: wandering, irrelevance, put-downs, negatives, overloads.
Aim for flexibility in communication skills, for clarity, listening, questioning,
     understanding; watch non-verbal behaviour and elicit any blocks.
Record what was said and check for understanding.

■ Going for the balance

If you decide to go for a new way of working, there are various flexible options. The one that suits you will depend on what your needs are. To help you choose the right balance for you, consider the following and decide your priorities:

more time at the beginning and/or end of the day
a free day during the week
school holidays

lower income

changes to employment rights, pension or holiday entitlement

career status and chances of promotion

job satisfaction

time to retrain

Use and adapt the following guidelines to help you prepare for any interviews, meetings, assessments and appraisals you might need to attend in connection with changing the way you work, for example with an employer, prospective employer, trainer or bank manager.

Preparation
Find out about your company's policy on flexible working. Review your career – don't assume that your record will be known and understood, or that it has been recorded accurately. Prepare a short CV to use if required.

The interviewer(s)
Do they have personal experience of your work and skills? Do prior relationships have to be taken into account?

Knowledge about you
What have recent appraisals said about you? What skills/strengths will be evident (or not)? Are there any negative aspects that will need explanation?

Your proposal for flexible working
Why are you making the proposal? What will this mean for your employer? How will changes affect the workplace/fellow workers? Will there be costs and/or savings? Will staffing levels be affected?

The decision
If offered less than you want, can you negotiate? Can you say no? Is there anyone you can use as a safe sounding board? Aim to get a constructive dialogue going with your employer. Listen. Aim to clarify: don't argue or defend. Respond with facts rather than opinions. Focus on the future – objectives, support, resources. Ensure that you understand the outcome.

In short:

relax

be succinct

be relevant

be confident

■ Your new status

Your employer may need to be assured of your continuing commitment to the job if you have gone on to flexi-time. If you've taken the independent route, you will have clients to satisfy instead of employers. Think about the following questions regarding your goals and motivation.

Q: What goals have you set for yourself:

a) in the short-term?

b) in the long term?

Q: Have you changed the working practices of yourself or your team lately? Can you give an example?

Q: If you are working shorter hours, how would you ensure that the small things still get done and checked?

Q: What does quality mean to you, in your work?

Q: Have you had any feedback on the quality of your work?

Q: How would you ensure that you meet all of your employer or clients' expectations? Give an example or two.

Do your answers show that you:

a) ensure your facts are accurate?

b) set up systems to ensure that you keep track of information?

c) attend closely to details?

d) monitor and check your work?

■ Flexible working

You may need to convince your employer that you intend to continue to:

    notice and act on opportunities;
    work without need of constant supervision;
    suggest when things could be improved upon;
    anticipate opportunities or problems;
    exceed job role descriptions;
    overcome obstacles and meet the end goals;
    involve others to make extraordinary efforts;
    persist and not give up if faced with problems.

Would you continue to:

    extend yourself to maintain a network of contacts?
    adjust your behaviour to meet the needs of others?
    anticipate the effect your behaviour has on others?
    'flex' your style to achieve desired result on others?
    make sure you are politically aware?
    make sure you manage stakeholders' interests?
    see the bigger picture?
    offer realistic compromises which balance views?
    give time to developing other people's skills?
    reinforce others' self-worth and self-value ?
    give honest feedback (i.e. about the behaviour, not the person)?
    give appropriately timed feedback (i.e. not 'off the cuff' or delayed)?
    keep a look out for opportunities to develop yourself and colleagues?
    give of your time considerably?
    share information readily?
    instill in others a sense of belief about their own potential?
    coach others to achieve goals?
    believe in consensual decision-making or common goals?
    like to share success ?
    promote a friendly and open climate in the team?
    work for win–win solutions?
    empower others?
    solicit ideas and opinions of others?

If you work independently for clients and you are proposing to reduce your hours, you may need to demonstrate how you would continue to meet their expectations. Think of two examples.

There are other questions you may find useful to consider too. What have you done to develop yourself over the last year? If there has been a major change in your organisation, how did it affect you? How do you see yourself working in one year's time? How do you see yourself working in five years' time? If you are staying with an organisation, how do you see your role there developing? Can you see the bigger picture? Can you think strategically, seeing how past, present and future actions are interlinked?

If you are staying with one organisation but working reduced hours, you will need to show that you intend to continue to be proactive even though you may be spending less time at work. The pursuit of work–life balance can relate to your deepest aspirations to develop and grow, make concerted and recorded effort in study, learn from experiences, adapt to the changing environment, approach problems from a constructive standpoint and carry out analysis intelligently and fairly.

Do you:

have a positive attitude to change?

anticipate and affect changes to improve performance?

develop and follow clear developmental goals?

approach problems from a constructive point of view?

never seek to blame?

take a systemic view of problems (seeing how one part relates to and affects all the others)?

Do you:

have a vision?

watch that your behaviour embodies the values of the vision?

communicate the vision?

deal with people fairly and equally?

encourage professional behaviour?

take responsibility for motivating your team?

show leadership in difficult times?

■ Maintaining professional standards

You will need to think about continuous professional development.

Would you:

keep up-to-date in your field?

seek further relevant development?

plan your contributions to meetings and projects?

integrate the work of professionals in your team?

ensure that your basic administrative and IT skills are kept relevant to your work?

understand and gain the necessary commercial skills for your field?

plan meetings: what you hope to achieve from the meeting?

consider what other people want to achieve from the meeting?

prepare your contributions: in meetings – make sure you know what is expected of you, your role, your status, group norms?

set an agenda, norms, manage air time, manage emotions, record minutes?

define and negotiate on targets, controls, information flow, administration?

understand what commercial skills are needed – and meet them?

ensure that you keep your technical and professional skills up-to-date?

By working through these questions you will have worked through a wide range of issues and developed your understanding of how you will approach them in your new role. This will enable you to be far more effective both in negotiating your plan, and in implementing it once you achieve your new status.

Having done this work in assessing yourself now and how you wish to be in the future, you may wish to do some reality checking with people who know you well so that you can test your understanding before you put it into practice.

Create a desirable future for yourself

Chapter 11
Motivation and decision-making

❑ Six basic motivating factors

❑ Marketing yourself

❑ Working out forces for and forces against

Years of social science research have identified six basic human requirements that must be present for people to be motivated and therefore effective. They are experienced differently from person to person. In relation to work–life balance, motivation is an essential factor in achieving a situation in which you can be both realistic and flexible in your planning for the future.

Factor 1: Space for decision-making

People need to feel that they are their own bosses, and that, unless in exceptional circumstances, they have room to make decisions they can call their own. On the other hand, they do not need so much elbow room that they don't know what to do.

Factor 2: Opportunity to learn on the job and go on learning

Learning is a basic human need. Even in leisure pursuits, people strive to constantly improve. Learning is possible only when people are able to:
    a) set goals that are reasonable challenges for them, and
    b) get feedback and results in time for them to correct their behaviour.

Factor 3: Variety

People need to be able to vary their work to avoid the extremes of boredom and fatigue. They need to set up a satisfying rhythm of work that provides enough variety and a reasonable challenge.

Factor 4: Mutual support and respect

People need help and respect from their co-workers, and to avoid conditions where they are pitted against each other so that one person's gain is another person's loss.

Factor 5: Meaningfulness

People need to be able tolerate what they do and what they produce should be socially useful. Meaningfulness includes both the worth and quality of a product and having a knowledge of the whole. Many jobs lack meaning because workers are such a small part of the final product that its meaning is denied them. Taken together, these dimensions make it possible for a person to see a real connection between their daily work and their broader social life.

Factor 6: A desirable future

This desirable future has work–life balance as a priority. It involves not necessarily a promotion but a career path that will continue to allow personal growth and increase in skills as well as less stress and more leisure time.

What's your score?

You might like to score your present situation/ideal work-life balance as follows. for the first three factors, score from -5 (too little) to +5 (too much) with 0 being just right. For the final three, score from 0 (none) to 10 (lots).

Factor	Score	
1 Room for decision making		
2 Opportunity to learn on the job and go on learning		
3 Variety		
4 Mutual support and respect		
5 Meaningfulness		
6 A desirable future		

■ Self-marketing

There are countless times when you are going to need to talk about yourself, and to leave the listener with a lasting, accurate and positive impression. To prepare an introduction that shows you in the best possible light, focus on these:

> What you have done that sets you apart from others
>
> What you do well
>
> How you like to do things
>
> What you contribute

Your aim is to say something comprehensive yet concise in a short time that will let the listener know not only what you do, but how you do it – in effect, what you bring to the business, the training or the group. Practise to refine a one-minute speech that succinctly says what you bring in a way that impresses people. To do this, you need a tape recorder.

1 Precis your growth as a person
2 Precis your strongest skills
3 Precis your highest achievements
4 Precis your most critical values
5 Write a paragraph pulling these together
6 Now say it into a tape recorder.
  (There is no other way to do this exercise.)
7 Listen to the recording of what you are saying: the content, the pace, the choice of words, the tone – does it represent what and how you contribute? Does it paint a picture of you?
8 Edit the speech to ensure you have the right balance. Practise again into a microphone. Polish it and refine it to no more than one minute.
9 Let a reliable friend or colleague listen to it, or practise it over the telephone to them.
10 USE IT. Try it out on people who will give you support. Practise it when you make introductions at parties, in the school playground, at meetings and note how it is received. It will give you a great sense of confidence when you open conversations at critical meetings.

■ How effective is your self-marketing?

Are you proud of your accomplishments and do you find ways of letting people know what they are? Do you seek feedback about your performance from colleagues, bosses, tutors and others? Do you use this feedback to improve your performance? Do you maintain contact with professionals in your field to make sure you know your value in the market-place and to help you determine trends in the field? Is your CV current, well-organised, concise and accurate? Does your CV reflect the measurable achievements of your career? Consider how you promote yourself and what you could do more effectively.

■ Making decisions

If you are faced with a difficult decision, try some decision-making tools to help ensure that you are making a wise choice. The challenge for us all is to stay flexible in our thinking, open to new and challenging ideas. We need to avoid getting trapped into the belief that our view is the only one that works.

As you learn to challenge and test your current mindsets, you will make dramatic positive changes to your life and the lives of those you care about. By engaging with this practice, you will overthrow old, inappropriate ways of doing things, leap ahead and get bags of energy and confidence.

■ Accepting and naming the problem

If you are on the way to making a decision to improve your work–life balance but feel that there are still problems, this exercise will help clarify the situation. Write down all that you sense to be a problem and the effect of each element. I've done a couple of examples for you.

Sense of the problem	Effect
At work from 7am to midnight	Tired
Personal finances not in good state	Timing not good to reduce hours

Can you use your senses (hearing, sight, touch, smell, taste) to come up with ideas about a problem and how to solve it?

1 How does it feel?

2 How does it smell?

3 How does it look?

4 What sound does it make?

5 What does it taste like?

■ Challenging assumptions

Assumptions underpin every decision you make, so it is often helpful to question them. Here is an easy way to question your assumptions:

Take this problem – a man who was running two profitable stores decided to open four more. He was newly married and they had an 8-month-old baby. The first two shops opened on time and were pulling in the expected income. His wife got pregnant again. The third store didn't open on time. The fourth was way behind schedule and the overall income from the stores plummeted. He relieved his stress by playing golf at weekends and football on Friday night.

Now, list all your assumptions about this problem.

Now, reverse all your assumptions. Your task is not to find 'a solution' to the problem but to recognise the limitations of solutions you might come up with when checked back against your assumptions.

Now look at your assumptions about a problem of your own.

First, name the problem. Then ask the questions:

What has stopped me sorting this earlier?

Why is that a problem?

How did I allow this situation to develop?

How have I reinforced/exacerabated it?

What is good about the situation that allowed it to get to this?

What would have to happen for this problem not to be a problem?

How else could I think about this?

Think about someone you admire from history, or a leader you respect, a grandparent, a teacher you loved. How would they see this?

Now, redefine the problem in terms of 'I need to…'

Look at your desired end state. It has to be motivational. Rework it if it isn't.

■ Generating alternatives – brainstorming

This process work best if you can involve someone you trust to play it with you, but you can do it alone.

List five insights and then create possible solutions to them. Make no judgements, discussion, criticism about any suggestion. All ideas, even absurd ones, are welcome and need to be recorded faithfully. The quantity of ideas is the major objective. Ideas can be combined and refined later.

■ Make your choice: force-field analysis

This is a method you can use to make a decision about your work–life balance by plotting the 'forces for' and 'forces against' a chosen course of action. It is a thorough way of working out the pros and cons and will help you to plan or reduce the impact of the opposing forces, and strengthen and reinforce the supporting forces.

You need pen and paper. First of all, be clear about what your chosen course of action is. Write it down at the top of the sheet. Then create two columns. To carry out the force-field analysis:

1 List all forces 'for change' in one column, and all forces 'against change' in the other column
2 Assign a score to each force, from 1 (weak) to 5 (strong).
3 Draw a diagram showing the forces for and against,and the size of the forces.

Once you have carried out an analysis, you can decide on the viability of your course of action. Here you have two choices:

To reduce the strength of the forces opposing a project.
To increase the forces pushing a project.

This will help you to weigh the importance of these factors and to assess whether a plan is worth pursuing. Where you have decided to proceed with a plan, carrying out a force-field analysis helps you identify changes that might be made to improve the plan.

If you were faced with the task of deciding whether to work part-time, say, the analysis could raise:

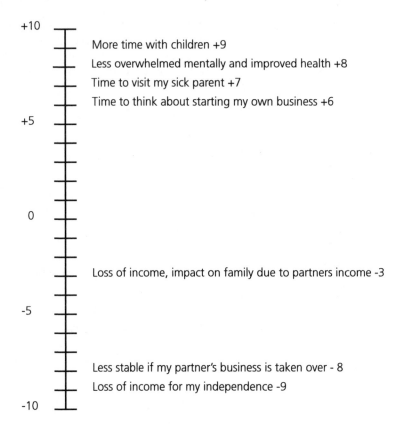

+10

More time with children +9
Less overwhelmed mentally and improved health +8
Time to visit my sick parent +7
Time to think about starting my own business +6

+5

0

Loss of income, impact on family due to partners income -3

-5

Less stable if my partner's business is taken over - 8
Loss of income for my independence -9

-10

Use this blank chart to plot the benefits and pitfalls of your plan.

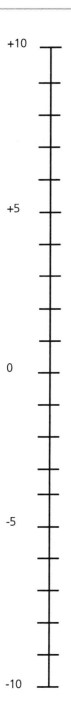

Balance works!

Chapter 12
Finding fulfilment

❏ Ask the right questions

❏ Focus on giving and sharing

❏ Cultivate flexibility and resourcefulness

❏ Be adaptable to change

Fulfilment might seem like light years away, even if you know what it is and how to get it. Ultimately, fulfilment is about connecting. It is about being able to give maximum attention and engagement to the things that are important to you. To achieve a better work–life balance the process of personal transformation is as important as working out where you want to be and why you want to be there. Be patient with yourself and others as you work towards your work–life balance, and remember that they are involved in their journey too.

The following accounts of how people found their work-life balance will inspire you. They will show that you can achieve what you set out to do and incorporate your core values into your plan.

Simon's story

Simon, a successful IT consultant, worked very long hours. His income rose every year. He kept old clients and was good at attracting new ones because of his enthusiasm, ideas and self-confidence. He had three children, whom he saw only on Saturdays because during the week he left home early and rarely returned before they were in bed. On Saturdays, however, he ensured he spent 'quality time' with them – in productive things, such as driving them to extra-curricular lessons of football, tennis, piano, remedial maths.

It seemed good on the surface – however, his life and that of his family was geared wholly towards achievement. It was all about what they'd achieved, won, nearly won, will win, own and have. He wrote goals for himself and his family every year, and there were conscious reminders for everyone on daily display. Planning his future was a question of creating a vision, planning and working to the plan, as well as spotting opportunities that arose around the plan. His life was totally goal-focused.

Recently, he overextended himself. He bought a house that was far too expensive because it was his dream, and became saddled with debt and unable to make ends meet effectively. Suddenly he had to face up to a need to reassess the way he lived. Debt became such a problem, affecting his wife and children just as much as him, that he was forced to take realistic measures to solve it.

In trying to work out a way forward for his family, Simon did a lot of soul-searching and recognised that he had been living according to a set of values that, in his heart, he didn't believe in. He realised things had to change. He sold the expensive property and moved to a smaller, more affordable house where his wife and children are happier. Because he doesn't have to work long hours in order to keep up the payments on his expensive home, he is able to spend more time with his wife and children. In this way, he turned his problem into an opportunity to achieve a work–life balance that suits him and his family.

Charles's story

Charles is an investment banker who until recently worked 12-hour days in an intense working environment. He has succeeded in renegotiating his hours so that he takes a day off each week to go to see friends or visit an art gallery. He believes the space has made him far more creative and that it enables him to do his job better with more energy. He is aware that it is a brave move in his very competitive area of work and is watching carefully to see if the result is that his career plateaus, which could affect his promotion prospects. If it does, he may have to reconsider, but for the moment it is working.

Natalie's story

Natalie runs a successful business. She loves her work, which is demanding, stimulating and challenging. She has a wide circle of friends and spends a lot of time with her three children. She can afford a good network of cleaners and assistants. Her stockbroker husband Nick is a kind, loving partner, but as he is absorbed in his own career, they have very little quality time together.

Natalie says she balances her work with her commitment as a mother and feels satisfied with that. She socialises with her friends and visits her ageing parents twice a month. However, her marriage is suffering because she and Nick have gradually lost touch with each other over the last 20 years while they have been putting all their energy into building their respective careers.

On the surface it seems to be a happy home with no arguments, no animosity and no resentments. Natalie and Nick hardly ever spend time enjoying each other's company, however, and now want different things out of life. Recently Natalie has persuaded Nick to face up to the fact that they have spent most of their married life not talking about what is truly important. There is a lot at stake so they are working at saving their marriage.

In any sustainable partnership, over time, you need to check that your partner is still the right one – that they support and encourage you. There must be give and take, on both sides. Like many other couples struggling to keep a family going and revitalise their marriage, they are in transition, and their situation has arisen essentially because of their lack of work–life balance over a long period of time.

Eve's story

Eve was a secretary working for a small business. She was efficient, bright, reliable and her boss offered her promotion. Eve turned it down because her life revolved around her husband and children. Her boss accepted her priorities but persevered in the offer and suggested a course in computer programming that could be done on-line, at home in the evenings. It would, if she completed it, allow Eve to move into a higher paid and more interesting job.

For a while Eve wondered whether to take up the opportunity because she was busy enough leaving work at 3pm to pick up the children and then looking after them and preparing the evening meal. It took her seven weeks to accept the offer. She didn't realise how pivotal it would be to her future security. That month someone knocked at her door declaring to be her husband's lover. Eve's world fell apart. She tried to work it out with her husband but within a year they separated. Suddenly and totally unexpectedly she was a single mother, whereas he, as she saw it, was a single man. He went off with the other woman, barely contacted the children and paid no maintenance until he absolutely had to.

Suddenly, she had to be the main breadwinner in the family. For a while she was terrified, angry, wondering if she could cope, but she did, and has rebuilt her home and family. Her children have been eased through the transition by her ability to communicate with them and build their confidence, and by their ability to co-operate with and help her.

The studies were put off for a year when there was just too much to do but now the children depend on her less, and she has more time on her hands. She is in the final stage of her training and can look forward to a rise and a role change in her employment. She faced her fear and realised it was false, and succeeded in creating a way of living that suits and works for her and the children.

Maria's story

Maria knew she wanted to work with maths since she was eight years old. By the time she was 12 she knew she wanted to be an engineer. She was ambitious and enthusiastic, and she became a very good engineer, working for one of the world's largest firms. She was given the chance to be chief architect and engineer for a major project. It was exactly the exciting, high-profile, complex project she had always dreamed of. There was one problem – it would mean travelling to the other side of the world and she had given birth to her third baby only four months earlier. It was a huge dilemma. She worked it out with her husband and left her children in the safe and loving hands of their father.

Maria's mother and her mother-in-law were unhappy about this arrangement. One Sunday they said, in front of the children, ' … poor little things, their mother hardly ever here.' Maria had to make her stand. She said, 'Don't you dare tell my children that. They have two parents. One was looking after them at that time, then later the other one did, and then both of us.'

Maria's children are proud of their mother and the family flourished. She said to me, 'Don't let others feel sorry for your kids because you are working' – remind them that they have a mother they are proud of who secures their financial safety and who shows them that life can be very fulfilling.

■ Personal fulfilment

It's important to acknowledge others in your life who have expectations of you, and to remember that they matter too. When you make changes, you may need to help others adjust their perceptions and expectations of you. All too often the commitment and absolute focus needed to achieve great things means that the needs of family, friends and sometimes colleagues take second place. If you take advantage of those closest to you, you will be dependent upon their constitution and their value system as to whether in the long run they will be there when you turn around again.

Feelings of personal fulfilment are often linked to other people's recognition of us, people's gratitude towards us. To give to others can provide the greatest sense of satisfaction and contentment because we've done something worthwhile.

Instead of searching for that elusive perfect relationship, that ideal career move, that certain something that will change your life forever, focus on giving and sharing if you want to feel fulfilled.

As part of your ongoing progress in work–life balance, make your intention to be kind, compassionate, helpful, creative, useful, to give pleasure – these are the ingredients that make up the feast of fulfilment. 'Why am I here?' is the question to ask because it will reveal your purpose – not 'what do I want out of life', which ultimately becomes an endless pursuit of more, bigger, better in order to find lasting satisfaction.

When you succeed in achieving a better work–life balance, one that suits you and those close to you, it will help you to remember that only change is constant. In focusing on improving well-being and levels of satisfaction, remember to acknowledge the reality of impermanence, ageing and changing priorities. If you continue to cultivate flexibility and resourcefulness, balance will always be possible to find.

Acknowledgements

Much of what I was able to write comes from the support and challenge I enjoy from the following people, for which I give thanks.

David Tom, for your kindness, your fatherhood and your good nature

Shirley John, for always being there, being on my side, your heart of gold and for being funny

Elaine North, my counsel, my right hand, my friend

Cyndi Robinson, for your gaiety, your gravitas and your graciousness

Angela Simmonds, always ready to live and to give

Janet Reibstein, for your empathy, beauty, fun

Beechy Colclough, for your verve, nerve and love

Robert Holden, for your reach, your work and friendship

Graham Alexander, for your subtle, provocative wit and wisdom

Morag Bramley, you are a mate, so cool, so capable

Paul McKenna, beyond the laughter you save lives, my friend

Michael Breen, so clever and talented, thank you for your faith

Millie McGough, you are one of the best

Godstowe School, for looking after our lovely girl

Antoni Kurr, for your help when I was stuck, you have a lot to offer

Soo Spector, for daring to be honest, for doing things right

Colletta, for your perspective and natural charm

Robert Kirby for being a dear and caring about me more than the project

Emma Shackleton for your sweet determination, calmness, vision

And others, who shall be nameless but are etched and embedded in my soul. You were there to lure me away from work and remember what life is about.

Further information

There is a lot of information on the World Wide Web about work–life balance and finding fulfilment. You may like to start with some of these websites:

www.bbc.co.uk/radio4/news/nicework
www.dti.gov.uk/work-lifebalance
www.freelancecentre.com
www.homeworkinguk.com
www.ivillage.co.uk
www.lifelearninginstitute.com
www.mentalhealth.org.uk
www.occenvmed.com
www.parentlineplus.org.uk
www.positivementalhealth.com
www.redcross.org.uk
www.smarterwork.com
www.teacher-training.net
www.vso.org.uk
www.workingbalance.co.uk

Further reading

Covey, Stephen R. *7 Habits of Highly Effective People*
Simon & Schuster 1999

Goleman, Daniel, *Emotional Intelligence: Why It Can Matter More Than IQ*
Bloomsbury 1996

Rowe, Dorothy *The Successful Self*
Harper Collins 1989

Warr, Peter *Psychology at Work*
Penguin 2002

More essential guides available in the Personal Development series from BBC Books:

*Get Up and Do It!: Essential Steps
to Achieve Your Goals*
Beechy and Josephine Colclough
Publication date: March 2004
ISBN: 0 563 48765 8
CD ISBN: 0 563 52346 8

*Starting Out: Essential Steps
to Your Dream Career*
Philippa Lamb and Nigel Cassidy
Publication date: August 2004
ISBN: 0 563 52140 6
CD ISBN: 0 563 52389 1

*The Confidence Plan: Essential Steps
to A New You*
Sarah Litvinoff
Publication date: March 2004
ISBN: 0 563 48763 1
CD ISBN: 0 563 52336 0

*Negotiation: Essential Steps
to Win in Your Work and Life*
Hugh Willbourn
Publication date: August 2004
ISBN: 0 563 52148 1
CD ISBN: 0 563 52394 8

*Be Creative: Essential Steps to
Revitalise Your Work and Life*
Guy Claxton and Bill Lucas
Publication date: March 2004
ISBN: 0 563 48764 X
CD ISBN: 0 563 52331 X

*Embracing Change: Essential Steps
to Make Your Future Today*
Tony Buzan
Publication date: January 2005
ISBN: 0 563 48762 3

All titles are available at good bookstores and online through the BBC Shop at www.bbcshop.com